Covert Manipulation

The Secrets, The Art of Reading, and Influencing People with Dark Psychology, Persuasion and Deception. Covert NLP, Brainwashing, and Mind Control

Text Copyright © [Robert Sinclair]

All rights reserved. No part of this guide may be reproduced in any form without permission in writing from the publisher except in the case of brief quotations embodied in critical articles or reviews.

Legal & Disclaimer

The information contained in this book and its contents is not designed to replace or take the place of any form of medical or professional advice; and is not meant to replace the need for independent medical, financial, legal or other professional advice or services, as may be required. The content and information in this book has been provided for educational and entertainment purposes only.

The content and information contained in this book has been compiled from sources deemed reliable, and it is accurate to the best of the Author's knowledge, information and belief. However, the Author cannot guarantee its accuracy and validity and cannot be held liable for any errors and/or omissions. Further, changes are periodically made to this book as and when needed. Where appropriate and/or necessary, you must consult a professional (including but not limited to your doctor, attorney, financial advisor or such other professional advisor) before using any of the suggested remedies, techniques, or information in this book.

Upon using the contents and information contained in this book, you agree to hold harmless the Author from and against any damages, costs, and expenses, including any legal fees potentially resulting from the application of any of the information provided by this book. This disclaimer applies to any loss, damages or injury caused by the use and application, whether directly or indirectly, of any advice or information presented, whether for breach of contract, tort, negligence, personal injury, criminal intent, or under any other cause of action.

You agree to accept all risks of using the information presented inside this book.

You agree that by continuing to read this book, where appropriate and/or necessary, you shall consult a professional (including but not limited to your doctor, attorney, or financial advisor or such other advisor as needed) before using any of the suggested remedies, techniques, or information in this book.

Table of Contents

INTRODUCTION	10
CHAPTER 1: WHAT IS COVERT MANIPULATION?	13
COVERT MANIPULATION	14
PERSUASION VS. MANIPULATION	15
KEY INFORMATION	18
EMOTIONS	18
EMPATHY	21
CHAPTER 2: HOW TO DISCOVER IF YOU ARE MANIPULATED	24
FEELING IGNORED OR UNIMPORTANT	26
CONSTANTLY DISADVANTAGED	27
FEELING FEAR, OBLIGATION, AND GUILT	28
SELF-DOUBT	30
FRIENDS AND FAMILY ARE CONCERNED	31
CHAPTER 3: HOW PEOPLE ARE MANIPULATED AND WHY	32
WHY PEOPLE MANIPULATE	33
SELFISH INTERESTS	33
DESIRE FOR POWER	34
BOREDOM	34
UNINTENTIONAL	35
MENTAL DISORDERS	35
PROCESS OF MANIPULATION	35
LEARN THE OTHER PERSON'S NATURE	37

BECOME A TRUSTED PERSON	37
WEAKEN SELF-ESTEEM	37
USE TECHNIQUES	38
COMMON MANIPULATION TECHNIQUES	**39**
DECEPTION	39
PLAYING THE VICTIM	42
ISOLATION	42
SEDUCTION	43
BLAME	43
FALSE PERSONA	44
DIVERSION	44
CHAPTER 4: SIGNS OF MANIPULATION	**46**
DEVELOPING DEPRESSION	**46**
DEVELOPING ANXIETY	**47**
DEVELOPING UNHEALTHY COPING MECHANISMS	**49**
CODEPENDENCY	**50**
DISHONESTY	**51**
LACK OF CARE FOR SELF	**52**
UNTRUSTING	**52**
LACK OF SELF-ESTEEM	**53**
CHAPTER 5: EMOTIONAL MANIPULATION TACTICS	**55**
UNDERSTANDING EMOTIONS FOR MANIPULATION	**55**
ANGER	56
FEAR	56
GUILT	57
SADNESS	58
STEPS TO EMOTIONAL MANIPULATION	**58**
CREATING EMOTIONS	59

EXPLOITING EMOTIONS	60
GASLIGHTING	**61**
LOVE BOMBING AND DEVALUING	**62**
SILENT TREATMENT	**64**
AGGRESSION OR ANGER	**65**
PASSIVE AGGRESSIVE COMMUNICATION	**66**

CHAPTER 6: INFLUENCE WITHOUT MANIPULATION	**68**
PRINCIPLES OF PERSUASION	**68**
RECIPROCITY	69
LIKABILITY	71
AUTHORITY	72
SOCIAL PROOF	73
SCARCITY	74
CONSISTENCY AND COMMITMENT	75
ETHOS, PATHOS, LOGOS	**75**
ETHOS	76
PATHOS	77
LOGOS	78
NEURO-LINGUISTIC PROGRAMMING	**78**
MIRRORING	79
ANCHORING	81

CHAPTER 7: MANIPULATION IN RELATIONSHIPS	**83**
SIGNS OF A MANIPULATIVE RELATIONSHIP	**85**
ACCUSATIONS	85
MIND GAMES	86
THINGS ARE CONSTANTLY DAMAGED	86
JEALOUSY	86
ALWAYS A VICTIM	87

Rushed into Decisions ... 88
Inconsistency Between Actions and Words ... 88
Constant Negotiation ... 88
Words Are Constantly Distorted ... 89
Effects of a Manipulative Relationship ... 89

CHAPTER 8: MANIPULATION IN THE WORKPLACE ... 91

Signs of Workplace Manipulation ... 92
You Feel Upset, Sad, or Depressed Around Someone ... 92
You Feel a Sense of Obligation to Someone ... 93
You Have Changed ... 94
You Find Someone in the Office Unpredictable ... 94
You Feel Devalued ... 95
Effect of Workplace Manipulation ... 95

CHAPTER 9: HOW TO ELIMINATE MANIPULATIVE PEOPLE ... 98

Know the Signs ... 99
Be Assertive ... 99
Avoid Suspected Manipulators ... 101
Never Give Up Values ... 102
Always Take Time to Consider Options ... 103
Learn to Say No ... 103
Ask if Request is Reasonable ... 105

CHAPTER 10: INTERMITTENT REINFORCEMENT ... 107

Defining Intermittent Reinforcement ... 107
Using Intermittent Reinforcement ... 108
Dangers of Intermittent Reinforcement ... 110

CHAPTER 11: TIPS AND TRICKS TO DEFEND YOURSELF FROM MANIPULATION — 114

- **CREATE AND UPHOLD BOUNDARIES** — 114
- **DEVELOP A SOLID SELF-ESTEEM** — 117
- **FOSTER STRONG RELATIONSHIPS** — 118
- **LEARN YOUR RIGHTS** — 119
- **REFUSE TO MAKE EXCUSES** — 121
- **SET CONSEQUENCES** — 121
- **REJECT BLAME AND PERSONALIZATION** — 122
- **MAINTAIN FLEXIBILITY** — 123

CONCLUSION — 125

Introduction

Congratulations on purchasing *Covert Manipulation*, and thank you for doing so.

In purchasing this book, you must have some sort of vested interest in learning about manipulation. Perhaps you were manipulated once by someone, and you are hoping to learn everything possible about the process in order to protect yourself in the future. Maybe you feel as if learning to manipulate or persuade others will be beneficial to you somehow. You could even be doing research for some sort of project, such as for a book you are trying to produce. Regardless of your reason for picking up this book, hopefully, you will not be disappointed.

As you read through this book, you will learn everything you need to know to develop an elementary understanding of what covert manipulation entails. You will learn about crucial background information that needs to be known prior to attempting to utilize anything within this book, such as understanding empathy or emotions, both of which are crucial to understanding how to control other people. You will learn many of the signs of being manipulated as well as how to recognize the process when you fall victim to it. You will learn about how people manipulate with emotions, and without learning the most common covert manipulation tactics, there are. You will learn about influencing others without manipulation, such as through persuasion or neuro-linguistic programming. You will see what manipulation looks like in both the workplace and in relationships, as well as develop an understanding of just how detrimental it can be to the environment within each. Finally, you will learn how to eliminate manipulation from your life, as well as how to defend yourself from falling victim to manipulation.

Remember, manipulation is not something to be taken lightly. In the wrong hands, it can absolutely be a weapon that, if not wielded responsibly, absolutely can cause irreparable harm to someone else's mind and life. In learning how to manipulate others, you are learning how to take control of their innermost thoughts and motivations, and for that reason, it should not happen without an important reason. The methods that will be discussed in this book are intended to be educational by nature and are designed to foster understanding, not to be used in unethical, harmful manners toward other people.

While there are several other books that touch upon the subjects of dark psychology and covert manipulation, your support in purchasing this book is deeply appreciated. This book is absolutely intended to be informational, providing you with as much information on the subject of covert manipulation as possible, organized as concisely as possible to be of the most useful to you.

Now, without further ado, you are ready to delve into the dark, alluring, and deeply enticing world of covert manipulation. The methods you will learn about will enable you to develop more nuanced control over people than you ever thought was possible. Please enjoy, and as you do, remember to utilize any techniques as responsibly as possible. Ultimately, the responsibility falls upon you to wield these techniques ethically and with good intentions.

Chapter 1: What is Covert Manipulation?

Have you ever been in a relationship in which you find yourself suddenly and inexplicably doing something you never imagined you would willingly do? You may suddenly stop to reevaluate and recognize that you are engaging in behaviors entirely foreign to you, such as speaking in a manner that is uncharacteristic to you or making decisions to do something for someone that inherently violate your own moral values. While you recognize that you find the behavior you are engaging in to be atypical of you, you cannot fight the urge to go through with it anyway.

If that sounds familiar, you may have been a victim of covert manipulation—manipulation meant to slip past your conscious detection to control your own conscious behaviors. The entire intention of covert manipulation is to get in, convince the other person to behave in the way you are intending, and sneak out, entirely undetected in the process. If you manage to do this, you are able to control the mind of someone else, and they will be none the wiser. By the time any changes in personality or behavior are noted, you will struggle to identify where the cause in change was, and you may even believe that the change was natural and reflected your emotional state and, therefore, should be trusted as legitimate.

Covert Manipulation

Covert manipulation is something that may sound complicated, but the concept is quite simple: It is manipulation that is covert. Through etymology, you can then assume that it is any form of manipulation that is meant to be secret or undetected. However, you may be wondering what counts as manipulation. Is asking someone to do something manipulation? Is convincing them to do so with legitimate facts or through logic manipulation?

Manipulation itself has several defining features that must be understood in order to get a solid grasp on the concept of covert manipulation. Manipulation is an intentional influence that is designed to control someone else or the thoughts of someone else through deceptive manners in order to get what you want. It is almost always exploitative or dishonest, hiding important aspects in hopes of convincing someone more successfully.

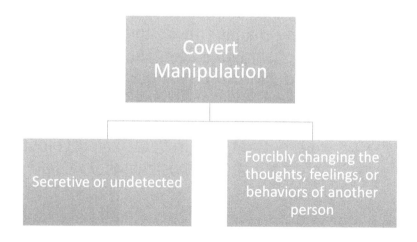

Most often, manipulation occurs because someone wants to feel powerful in his or her relationship, someone wants to use someone else as a stepping stone to get what he or she wants, boredom and wanting to play games, or simply accidentally doing so due to struggling to understand human interaction. It is not always intentionally done just to hurt someone else, though someone getting hurt is frequently an unintended consequence—more often, someone getting hurt is nothing more than collateral damage as the manipulator uses the other person as a means to an end. When it is unintentional, however, it is usually a symptom of either disordered thinking or of someone else's lack of empathy or understanding of emotions. Regardless, the effects are largely the same, and those who have been victimized by covert manipulation frequently feel the same—violated.

Persuasion vs. Manipulation

While persuasion and persuasive techniques, such as appealing to the principles of persuasion may be considered influential in the sense that they are meant to change the mind of another person, it is important to understand that not all social influence is a form of manipulation, and not all forms of influence are as harmful as manipulation. In fact, influence through persuasion can often be a good thing—persuasion seeks to change the mind of someone else while also being forthright and recognizing that an individual's right to free will. Sure, the result may be the same—you convince the other person to change his mind. However, the intention matters here.

In manipulation, the victim is quite frequently unintended to be harmed. The harm is not meant to happen, but the manipulator does not care about it happening in the first place. Of course, this is problematic in its own way. Humans ought to never be treated as nothing more than means to various ends, meaning they should never be used as little more than stepping stones with no regard to their own emotional states or willingness to go along with the process. It is always important to understand that people have thoughts, feelings, and rights, and manipulation frequently tries to override that altogether.

When you want to understand the difference between manipulation and persuasion, or you are not sure if what you are engaging in is manipulation or persuasion, there is a relatively simple technique you can use to analyze your behaviors. All you will need to do is spend some time considering a few different questions and use your answers to determine if what you are doing is manipulative or persuasive in nature.

First, you must identify what your intentions are. Ask yourself why you intend to sway the mind of someone else. Is it for yourself, or is it more altruistic? Of course, the answer to this is largely based on your own ethics and moral code and is never black or white. However, if what you are doing is largely self-serving or underhanded, it is likely that what you are engaging in is manipulation rather than persuasion.

Next, ask yourself whether you have been honest with the other person or if you have been trying to hide or misrepresent any information that could be crucial in making an informed decision. If you are being secretive and deliberately withholding information because you know it will have an impact on the decision contrary to what you want to happen, you are quite possibly being manipulative. On the other hand, full disclosure and honesty oftentimes imply persuasive methods rather than manipulative.

Lastly, consider who benefits from this attempt to change someone's mind. If the one being convinced to change does not benefit at all, or benefits somewhat, but disproportionately to how much you stand to benefit, it is likely that your behavior is manipulative. If the other person is largely benefitting from the process, regardless of how much you are benefitting as well, it is possibly persuasion.

Remember, you must consider all three questions in conjunction with each other to get a full picture. It is possible for something you are doing to be beneficial to the other person but still be manipulative. It is possible that you have been honest, but you are only doing so in order to benefit yourself, making the process more manipulative than persuasive. It is possible that your honesty was accompanied by threats or attempts to intimidate or coerce a reaction. No matter what, always consider the above three points to get a good idea of whether you are manipulative or persuasive.

Manipulative	Persuasive
• Selfish or malicious intent	• Selfless or innocent intentions
• Dishonest or lack of transparency in information	• Complete honesty and transparency
• Manipulator primarily benefits	• One being swayed primarily benefits
• Typically coercive or exploitative	• One being persuaded is making changes of his or her own volition

Key Information

As you progress in this book, you will need to understand two key concepts: Emotions and empathy. These two concepts are used repeatedly in controlling the minds of others, as both are major behavioral motivators in humans. Because both empathy and emotions are so incredibly intrinsically motivating, it becomes incredibly important to really understand them; if you are able to subtly control the emotions of others or prey on someone else's empathy, you will be able to engage in far more influencing of others than you may have thought you were capable of.

Emotions

Emotions are a driving force for everyone. They are the mind's way of motivating the body into behaving in certain ways. The brain has to process any and all sensory input, grapple with thoughts, and then create the impulses that create behavior. It does this through emotions—strong, sudden, urges, or feelings that drive the individual feeling them to do something conducive to survival. The emotions are the brain's way of communicating back to the body in a way the body can understand. It feels the changes in the physical state that prime the body to respond accordingly, and the person then is able to react.

If you had to define emotions, it would be an instinctive state of mind created in response to sensory stimuli. These states of mind are not rational—they are intuitive and automatic. They do not have to be learned or taught through experience and are instead simply felt no differently than how people feel hunger or thirst to motivate them to eat or drink.

We have several different emotions that encourage different behaviors and communicate different needs to those around us, with seven recognized as universal: happiness, sadness, fear, surprise, contempt, anger, and disgust. Each of these does something to aid in survival.

Emotion	Purpose
Happiness	• Conveys comfort and that needs are met • Encourages repeating behaviors that caused it
Sadness	• Conveys loss or harm and need for support • Encourages avoiding repeating past mistakes
Fear	• Conveys danger and need for protection • Prepares body for fight-or-flight
Surprise	• Conveys not expecting something and need for attentiveness • Allows senses to take in more information
Contempt	• Conveys hatred or disapproval and need for space • Allows for expression of disapproval
Anger	• Conveys feeling threatened and need for boundaries • Encourages aggression and protective behaviors
Disgust	• Conveys feeling something is toxic and need to avoid • Encourages avoidance and protects sense organs

Emotions that are felt, then, serve two major purposes: they motivate, and they communicate. These allow for survival in several ways—in preparing your body to tackle any circumstances, you are able to better survive and take care of yourself, and in being able to communicate your feelings at any given moment through body language and expressions, you are able to ensure that others help you meet any needs that you cannot meet yourself through empathy.

Empathy

Empathy is directly related to emotions—empathy refers to the capacity to feel the emotions of another person. When you are able to empathize with someone, you know how they feel—you have a direct understanding of the other person's emotional state, and you are able to cue in on that emotional state. Some people understand it at a fundamental level through cognitive empathy, in which they are aware of the states of others, but others understand it more intimately; they pick up on the emotional state of others, taking on the feelings as if they were their own in something known as compassionate empathy. When cognitive and emotional empathy combine, they create what is known as compassionate empathy. This has a very specific biological function—empathy encourages selfless behavior through communication.

In the wild, selfless behavior is oftentimes quite negative; if only some people have a tendency toward selfless behavior, they are not going to survive very long. However, when the vast majority of the population has selfless tendencies, engaging in sharing of food or responsibilities when necessary, the entire group as a whole is more likely to survive. Think of the expression, "It takes a village," and you start to see how. When you are willing to behave selflessly, you are able to engage in all sorts of counterintuitive behaviors—you may share your food with a neighbor who does not have any. You may decide to help someone else catch up on work even though it will eat up your time for rest. These selfless behaviors not only help other people survive but also encourage other people to behave selflessly as well, which directly improves your chances of being on the receiving end of that selflessness at a point where you desperately need it to survive. After all, if you face a time of struggling, those that you have helped are going to feel more inclined to help you in return due to one specific way of thinking: Reciprocity. Reciprocity refers to one of the principles of persuasion, which will be discussed in more detail in Chapter 6: Influence without Manipulation.

Empathy is relevant to manipulation for one specific reason: it is motivating. It is entirely possible for manipulators to prey on the empathy of those around them, cueing into it and ensuring that the other party feels bad for them. In making sure the other person is empathetic, it becomes far easier to influence the other person because you can use that empathetic nature to your own advantage. You can create situations in which empathy allows you to sway the emotions of the other party, creating certain emotions to encourage certain reactions. The more empathetic the target is, the easier it becomes to sway the other person through emotional means. Typically, empathetic individuals, often known as empaths, are far more willing to put up with behaviors that are negative simply because their empathy allows them to see into the hearts of other people, understanding their intrinsic motivators, and when they can follow that line of logic, they become more likely to actively put up with manipulative behavior, feeling as though they can change the manipulator.

Chapter 2: How to Discover if You Are Manipulated

Because manipulation can be so incredibly tricky to identify, it often goes entirely undetected. Particularly in the case of covert manipulation, the entire purpose is for the process to escape detection, and unless you are well-versed in some of the most subtle warning signs, you are likely to fall victim to the tactics of a manipulator. These signs are crucial to know if you have ever fallen victim to a manipulator in the past, particularly because people who were victimized by manipulation in the past are frequently victimized in the future as well, due to sharing some of several traits that make an individual attractive as a target of manipulation.

Manipulators love people that possess five key similarities, as they create a much easier target for manipulation than others. These traits, while many can be incredibly useful in social settings, can also be used in the worst interest of the individual. These traits include:

- **Overly-trusting:** People who are trusting will often give others the benefit of the doubt, even when it is unwarranted. They will repeatedly give manipulators chances to prove themselves, even at their own detriments.
- **Empathetic:** People who are empathetic are easily swayed by those who want to control them. They

can be pushed to be angry, afraid, happy, or anything else simply through emotional appeals.

- **Codependent:** People who are codependent feel as though they cannot exist without their relationships, and because of that, they often feel they have no choice but to put up with any and all abuse given to them.

- **Conflict-avoidant:** When people become conflict-avoidant, they are willing to put up with all sorts of negative or manipulative behaviors simply because they would rather put up with it if putting up with it means they do not have to argue or confront someone.

- **Troubled past/upbringing:** When someone has a troubled, dysfunctional upbringing, they often never learned what a healthy lifestyle looks like. Rather than noticing red flags in relationships and behaviors, they assume the behaviors they saw in their childhood are normal. Yelling, manipulation, and even physical and verbal abuse can be normalized, meaning they are willing to put up with the worst behaviors.

Those traits create the perfect storm of someone who is easily targeted for manipulation, and because they hold those traits, they are frequently sought out specifically to be manipulated. Understanding these traits is important to recognize the kinds of people likely to be manipulated. If you have these traits, it is a sign that you should look to see if you are being manipulated yourself.

Feeling Ignored or Unimportant

When you are in a relationship with a manipulator, frequently, you are being targeted simply because you make a complacent target that is not likely to resist much. You may not even realize that you are being manipulated, though you know that you are unhappy in the relationship. When this happens, you need to stop and consider why you are feeling unhappy in the first place. Oftentimes, that unhappiness is rooted in feeling as though you are unimportant. You may feel ignored or as if your own opinions are completely irrelevant. If your preferences are never considered, you have a good reason to believe that you are, in fact, being manipulated.

Stop and consider whether your partner, friend, coworker, boss, or whomever it is you feel may be manipulating you, actually, do consider your likes and dislikes. It is one thing to compromise and agree to do something you would prefer not to, at least sometimes, but you should also have times in which you are getting what you want or need rather than relenting to whatever it is the other person wants.

Beyond compromises and getting your wants and needs met, do you feel as though you are actively being listened to? The manipulator does not care about his victim's feelings—all that matters to the manipulator is getting his way at the end of the day. If what you are saying is oftentimes cut off by the other person, at which point he or she changes the topic altogether, you may be in the vicinity of a manipulator. Someone who makes you feel unimportant or as though your thoughts, feelings, or beliefs are lesser is oftentimes using you rather than actually interested in you.

Constantly Disadvantaged

Because manipulators are almost always seeking out extra control over other people, it is oftentimes the case that they are actively seeking out ways in which they can regain the upper hand. Most frequently, this is through tactics that allow for a "home-court advantage," meaning the situation is largely controlled by the manipulator. If you feel as though you are constantly out of your element when interacting with the individual, it is possible you are being manipulated or controlled.

The manipulator may constantly invite you to parties at his house, or places he frequents, and if you try to reciprocate the invitation or invite the other person to spend time with you in your home environment, you are declined. This is because doing so grants the manipulator far more control over the situation and you than expected. You are exposed to what the manipulator wants to expose you to, and the manipulator, if he is good at what he does, will make sure he exposes you to only situations and events that would be beneficial to him.

This has a second level to it as well—when you feel out of your element, you are more likely to lean on the manipulator's familiarity and expertise. You will default to whatever the manipulator is saying or doing, and you will follow his lead. You are left in a position of vulnerability in which you are unsure of what to do next, and when people do not know what to do in a situation, they oftentimes will default to what their peers are doing, and in that situation, your peer is likely the manipulator. The manipulator is aware of this tendency, whether he is intentionally or unintentionally using it, and because he knows of the tendency, he will make it a point to keep you out of your own element to keep you complacent.

Feeling Fear, Obligation, and Guilt

These three feelings are closely intertwined and most frequently are used together in order to control other people. When someone is manipulating you, you are oftentimes obliging whatever the manipulator is pushing for because of one of three reasons—you feel fear, obligation, or guilt. While all three are healthy emotions some of the time, and they each serve incredibly important purposes in healthy relationships and situations, you must also keep in mind that they can become weaponized by a master manipulator, and when the master manipulator discovers the key to these three feelings, he discovers the key to your own behaviors.

Fear is a motivating emotion—it exists to encourage you to protect yourself in any way possible. You may prepare to run away if running gives you the best opportunity at success. You may prepare to fight if you are in a position where you cannot run, or if you are in a situation in which protecting yourself seems to be more conducive to survival. You may even freeze up in fear if the fear is overwhelming, giving the individual carte blanche to overrule anything you are doing or saying, and you are likely to follow along due to not knowing what else to do.

Obligation is a motivator to do what is right or expected. When you are obligated to something or someone, you feel an intense drive to follow through with whatever is expected. For example, humans frequently feel an intense obligation to take care of their children. That obligation is what makes parents wake up at all hours of the night to ensure that their children are fed and clean, particularly in the baby years in which the children cannot care for themselves. That obligation can be incredibly motivating for the individual. Of course, this obligation can be created in several different ways: the principle of persuasion known as reciprocation is relevant to creating an obligation. Empathy can create feelings of obligation as the individual often feels a moral obligation to alleviate any negative or harmful emotions being felt in the other party. Familial relationships can be used to encourage obligation, as oftentimes, we are taught from an early age to take care of our family. Another way to create obligation is through the persuasive principle of consistency and commitment. All of these instances can create the motivation to do things, even if they are things you would rather avoid doing in the first place.

Guilt is the result of an obligation that has been unfulfilled. It is meant to feel bad in order to encourage the individual to do better and avoid failing future obligations. The guilt essentially magnifies the feelings of obligation, and they can be used to coerce other people into fulfilling obligations. This is the birth of emotional manipulation such as guilt-tripping—the entire purpose is to use guilt to push people to do things they do not want to do by appealing to their sense of obligation.

Self-Doubt

Manipulators love to make people feel like they are crazy. They are able to do so through techniques like triangulation and gaslighting, both of which can lead to the victim of manipulation feeling as though he or she is actually in the wrong and confused about the entirety of the situation at hand. Oftentimes, the individual is left so convinced that the perception of reality is wrong that he or she instead defers to the beliefs or recommendation of the manipulator.

Of course, that is exactly what the manipulator wants; the manipulator wants to be in a position of power in which he is able to control the situation. If the individual constantly doubts herself, the manipulator has an easy in—the manipulator becomes a sort of beacon for the victim to follow; a guiding light, but rather than guiding the victim to safety, the manipulator does so to trap the victim in a perilous web of lies and deceit.

If you get to the point that you constantly feel as though your own perceptions of reality cannot be trusted, it may be time to re-evaluate. Ask those around you whether your perception is skewed, and make sure you ask more than one person. In only asking one person, you may actually be asking the manipulator, and the manipulator is not likely to tell you the truth. By asking several people, you can ensure that you get an honest interpretation.

Friends and Family are Concerned

It can be easy to brush off the opinions of friends and family as biased and too harsh, but they deserve some consideration, particularly if you find that your loved ones are constantly voicing negative opinions. Sure, it could be easy to push them away, and sure, people sometimes voice opinions that are intended to put a wedge between two people for selfish reasons, but far more regularly, when you have several friends and family members that are voicing concerns, it is often for a legitimate reason that at the very least deserves addressing. While it may be a hard pill to swallow that some of your friends or family may dislike someone you want in your life, if they dislike the other person, they probably are seeing red lags that you are missing somewhere. Considering that most of the time, loved ones only want what is best for you, you should take a look at what is happening and try to see through their eyes, at least for a little bit. Remember, your empathy is your biggest asset, and it can absolutely prove to be beneficial if you are being told by several people that there are problems in a relationship in your life.

Chapter 3: How People are Manipulated and Why

Once you have been targeted for manipulation, several different processes occur. The manipulators have a series of steps they must do in order to really establish an individual as a viable target of manipulation. Though there are several different techniques for manipulation, they require the same steps to first prime the target. Manipulators have no qualms about this—in fact, there are three criteria that must be met in order to be an effective manipulator in the first place. Manipulators must conceal their intentions, know the vulnerabilities of another person, and be ruthless enough to not care about the end result.

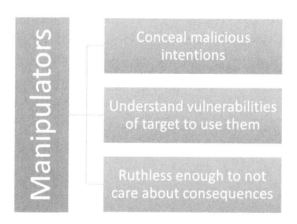

Why People Manipulate

People manipulate for several reasons. Despite their reasons for manipulating, the end result is the same: Someone ends up used as little more than a tool, a means to an end that does not actually matter in the grand scheme of things. The manipulator does not recognize basic human rights, such as the right to free will or the right to be respected. Instead, the manipulator only cares about controlling the other person for some reason. The reason does not have to be disclosed—what matters is that there is some motivation behind the manipulation that causes the techniques performed to be intended to get what he or she wants.

In using people as tools, someone always loses his or her humanity—they are no longer acknowledged as a human deserving of respect or having preferences, and instead, he or she is declared little more than a stepping stone. Using someone as a means to an end is belittling and can be incredibly destructive to an individual's view of him or herself. Take the time to familiarize yourself with several of the reasons an individual may take it upon himself to manipulate another person.

Selfish Interests

A common cause of manipulation is selfishness. The individual sees the target a roadblock to be conquered in order to get to what he or she wants, and the individual is willing to do whatever it takes to get to the desired end. They frequently then result in manipulation attempts, seeking to turn that roadblock into a tool or asset that could actually aid in the achievement of whatever was desired in the first place. This is essentially a little more than using an individual as a tool and is not recommended.

Desire for power

Sometimes, people want power. They may believe that they are deserving of that power and therefore act in methods that enable them to take it, or they may want to feel in control. They may even feel as though gaining that control over others will help their own self-esteem, and they seek to use people to boost their own egos. Nevertheless, people end up used as a tool and treated poorly in order to control them.

Boredom

Some people are motivated by boredom. They see the conquering of other people as little more than a game, and they will go out of their way to play just to break the monotony of reality. These people are toying with people without any clear objective other than seeing just how far they can push to get desired results.

Unintentional

Sometimes, the manipulation is entirely unintentional. These people may have picked up on manipulative actions or behaviors through years of being surrounded by it and think it is normal, much like how some people have grown up around dysfunction and come to expect it as normal. These people are not intentionally hurting people, but rather have grown up thinking their behaviors were normal in relationships.

Mental Disorders

Some people manipulate because they have mental health disorders that directly impact just how successful they are at actually relating to people. This role encompasses people like narcissists, psychopaths, and those with a Machiavellian personality trait. These three traits are known as the dark triad—a trio of behavioral traits that are incredibly destructive and do nothing but cause harm. These people are manipulative by nature without thinking about it and without intending to be— they manipulate because their brains are hardwired to prey upon people.

Process of Manipulation

Just as there are several reasons that someone may use manipulation, there are several techniques to doing so as well. However, these techniques require you to prime your target, so to speak. After all, you need to weaken the other person's resolve, making yourself trusted enough that your behaviors are not suspicious, in order to successfully manipulate someone. You need the other person to be unsuspecting and assuming that you are not, in fact, going to be manipulating other people. If you attempted to manipulate someone you were not close to in ways that were more emotional or obvious, it is not likely you would get very far simply because you would not have the rapport necessary to develop the influence necessary. For that reason, anyone attempting to manipulate usually begins through learning about the target they would like to manipulate, becoming a trusted person to that target, weakens the individual's self-esteem over time, and then finally begins using the manipulative techniques they have identified as being the most successful for the individual. Remember, manipulation is not easy, nor is it quick or meant to be used lightly. Manipulation is absolutely a long game, in which you plan out your steps and are frequently several steps ahead of your victim.

| Learn about your target | Earn your target's trust | Sabotage your target's self-esteem | Use manipulation techniques |

Learn the Other Person's Nature

The first step to manipulating someone is identifying your target and getting to know them. You need to learn as much as possible about the person. How do they behave regularly? What kind of support network do they have that would make manipulation attempts difficult or impossible? How well can you reasonably manage this individual? This is when you identify whether someone is going to be a reasonable target or a challenge.

Become a Trusted Person

Next, you need to become trusted somehow. You can do this by legitimately attempting to foster a relationship or through manipulative techniques like mirroring to fool the other person into feeling a relationship or love bombing, in which you essentially manipulate the other person into falling in love with you through addicting them to the feelings they have with you. No matter what, you need to establish yourself as trustworthy to the individual in order to move on to the real heavy manipulative techniques.

Weaken Self-Esteem

When you are trusted, you can begin chipping away at the individual's self-esteem. You can do this with small comments made to the other person that are ambiguous and will enable you to lie about your true intentions behind what you have said. For example, you could deny that when you said your target needed to try eating a salad that you mean that the other person needed to lose weight, and instead, you were trying to imply that the other person should try out this salad you had tried recently because you thought it was delicious and assumed the other person would think so too. Notice how you spun around a snide comment into something that was thoughtful on your part, leaving the individual feeling as he or she tries to figure out why the comment was upsetting when it was innocent. Over time, however, the individual's self-esteem will degrade, and as it erodes, the individual will be properly primed for manipulation.

Use Techniques

This is where the actual manipulation happens—thus far, you have been preparing the individual to be accepting of your mind control. Remember, to get this far, you have spent time legitimately fostering a relationship and legitimately, but subtly eroding the individual's mindset, and all of that takes time. However, you will start seeing results here. At this point, the individual is largely vested in your relationship, whether it is platonic or romantic, or even professional, and he or she is going to desire to stay on your good side. This means that your techniques are even more effective at this point because the individual will be scrambling to get back into your good graces as soon as there is a conflict, enabling you to begin effectively controlling them.

Common Manipulation Techniques

While the people who manipulate have no distinctive physical features, their manipulation attempts largely follow very similar patterns. Even manipulators who did not go out of their ways to learn techniques to manipulate often follow very similar structures to their manipulation. They engage in very specific techniques that resemble the techniques of other manipulators as if they have figured these techniques out naturally through trial and error. This section will list some of the most common forms of manipulation utilized by those seeking utter control and domination over their targets.

Deception

Deception is any sort of behavior that is meant to hide or obscure the truth behind something false. It can take several different forms, and most often occurs because the individual manipulating the other has something to gain from avoiding telling the truth. It can happen through saying things that are not true, concealing things, getting others to advocate for your cause, or even propaganda.

Deception comes in several different forms, with a wide range of people utilizing it. In fact, this is commonly used in politics when people do not want to tell the truth, or they want to skew things just enough to not look as bad as they know it will if they told the truth. Sometimes, it is used in relationships and sales pitches, as well. There are several different forms of deception, including the following:

- **Lying:** When people lie, they are deliberately stating things that are false. The things being said may have absolutely no bearing on the truth in any way and are frequently entirely untrue. This is telling someone that the reason you are late for work is because of a massive car crash on the highway that you had to stop for to present yourself as a witness, when in fact, you are late because you slept through three alarms after a night of partying a bit too hard.

- **Untruthful information:** When you are untruthful, you are usually misinterpreting the truth. What you are saying may be somewhat related to what the truth is, but you are still largely lying about the process. For example, you may say that most people disagree with some local law that is trying to be passed, when in fact, most people disagree because you interviewed only people that were opposed in the first place and you did not take a proper sample that would have shown a more legitimate skew in beliefs.

- **Equivocations:** When you say something that is indirect or ambiguous to avoid directly answering the question truthfully in the form that you were asked, you are engaging in equivocations. For example, you may play on the meaning of words with multiple meanings in order to skew the meaning. For example, once upon a time, sugar companies used to advertise their products as crucial and essential to the body because sugar is involved in several different bodily functions, neglecting to specify the difference between table sugar, or sucrose, and blood sugar, or glucose. Yes, both sucrose and glucose are sugars, but ultimately, what your body needs is glucose, which can be attained through several methods that do not require the consumption of sucrose.

- **Concealments:** Concealments refer to deliberately neglecting to mention entire portions of the truth or attempting to hide the truth, or to hide information that would be relevant to the situation at hand. For example, if you are selling a car with a stereo system that does not work and you know the brakes and engine will need servicing, and someone asks you if anything is wrong with it, answering, "It runs fine," would be your way of concealing the truth.

- **Exaggerations:** When you exaggerate, you make it a point to stretch the truth in order to serve your purpose better. For example, if a neighbor's puppy playfully nipped you and broke through your skin, you may exaggerate by saying that your neighbor's vicious dog charged at you and attacked.

- **Understatements:** Understatements are the direct opposite of exaggerations: when you understate something, you attempt to downplay the truth. Downplaying an instance could be a dog owner saying that their puppy was only playing after a brutal attack on another dog that was being walked by someone. The owner of the attacking dog may try to make an understatement, phrasing things as though his puppy playfully nipped at someone when, in fact, it was an adult dog that attacked aggressively.

Playing the Victim

When playing the victim, manipulators frequently attempt to convey things in such a way that they are actually the victim of a crime or wrongdoing rather than being the instigator. Manipulators are frequently masters of this, managing to flip the situation around and becoming worthy of sympathy in order to downplay what has happened and ensure that they are not seen as at fault. While many manipulators are out for power, they are not afraid of doing something like this in order to avoid losing control of a situation. While they may not seem outwardly powerful in this instance, they are still satisfied with being seen as deserving of sympathy to get what they want.

Isolation

Oftentimes, manipulators will slowly and systematically dismantle the entire support systems of their targets. Slowly, they will remove the support that their victims had, occasionally befriending the support themselves, while other times were engaging in behaviors that will put wedges between the victim and the victim's support. By removing that support, the victim is going to have fewer safeguards against manipulation in general. Because there will be no one there to point out how the manipulative behaviors are red flags due to no one being close enough to do so, the victim is kept under tight wraps, which also enables the manipulator to hide any manipulative behavior from becoming common knowledge.

Seduction

Sometimes, manipulators will go through seduction, essentially convincing someone else that they are, in fact, interested in the manipulator in order to get the desired results. This is usually done through manipulative behaviors such as love bombing or telling the victim exactly what the victim wants to hear to make the seducer more attractive.

Blame

Oftentimes, manipulators will use blame in order to scapegoat the individual they are manipulating. They will make it appear as though the legitimate problem is the victim, finding ways to make the victim being at fault plausible. The most common example is blaming the victim for any abuse that has been endured, telling the victim that he or she deserved it all because he or she brought it on. For example, if your partner cheats on you, he may claim that it is your fault because you did not satisfy his needs enough, and he had no choice but to go out and satisfy his need elsewhere.

False Persona

This is one particularly used by narcissists and those attempting to seduce others—in creating a false persona, one essentially creates a new personality that is unique to what the other person they are trying to victimize is interested in. For example, if their victim wants someone kind and thoughtful, the manipulator will be kind and thoughtful—until the façade becomes too exhausting and can be dropped.

Diversion

Manipulators using diversions or distractions usually distract those around them who are getting close to the truth. For example, imagine you just stole your roommate's last piece of cake. Your roommate was angered by your blatant disrespect for his property, understandably so, and in response, you decided to deflect the blame. You point out that your roommate has been stealing your shampoo the entire time you have lived together, and that it is not okay with you any longer either, even though you know that no one has been stealing your shampoo; you literally only say it to deflect blame and change the subject. Now, your roommate is so busy attempting to argue that he never touched your soap that you avoid the argument blaming you for the cake you ate.

Chapter 4: Signs of Manipulation

When you are being manipulated, it is crucial you know several of the signs. You have already been guided through the process of learning to identify when you may have been a victim of manipulation and red flags worthy of attention, but that was not an extensive list—there are also several other signs of manipulation that can occur. Many of these may slip under your radar, but through learning these telltale signs that you are being manipulated, you will be able to better protect yourself in a wide range of situations and circumstances. This is crucial—it gives you the ability to protect yourself. These are the most common side effects to being manipulated by someone, and understanding them can help you identify where the weak link in your relationship is in order to identify the manipulator and ensure that it comes to an end as soon as possible.

Developing Depression

Many times, those who are manipulated, particularly in longer-term situations, become depressed. Depression is characterized as a sad or depressed affect in which one frequently loses the ability to enjoy or engage in activities that were once pleasurable. The symptoms can cause feelings of guilt or worthlessness, both of which can be exacerbated when being manipulated. After all, manipulation is strongly dependent on guilt and feelings of inadequacy to get its point across.

The individual being manipulated is also at a higher risk for lack of energy or purpose, feeling so lost due to a lack of care for him or herself. After all, when one is the target of manipulation, he or she is most frequently taught that personal needs are irrelevant, and the needs of the manipulator must come first. Manipulation can also sometimes come with abuse and threats, both of which can increase the likelihood of depression.

If someone around you develops depressive symptoms shortly after a new relationship has been fostered, you should absolutely investigate. It is entirely possible that the new relationship is responsible for feelings of depression and a lack of interest in life in general. These symptoms need to be treated by a medical professional, and may even require therapy long-term, or medication in order to treat it. Keep in mind that these symptoms can be incredibly pervasive and can have massive impacts on one's life—they could lose jobs, lose relationships, and even begin developing impulses to self-harm or commit suicide, both of which are no laughing matter and should be reported to authorities as soon as they are noted.

Developing Anxiety

Anxiety also may arise as an unintended consequence of manipulation. Anxiety is a pervasive feeling of being in danger, feeling a sense of imminent threat, demise, or death, even though there may not be any legitimate dangers in the area at that particular time. This is largely related to the fact that many manipulation tactics rely largely on making the other person doubt him or herself, encouraging feelings of not knowing if their own minds are trustworthy, and in doing so, the individual feels that constant sense that something is going wrong or needs to be changed.

Because so much of manipulation hinges upon doubt, guilt, and quite possibly threats of some sort, the individual may develop anxiety as a consequence of so long walking on eggshells in an attempt to please the manipulator. If the manipulator is effective at his or her job, then the victim strongly feels a need to please the manipulator, and failing to do so can quickly be associated with anxiety, especially if the manipulator's response to failure is some sort of punishment.

Those with anxiety are largely characterized as having physical symptoms, such as higher blood pressure, trembling, quick pulses, and even dizziness. Beyond that, it is an emotional state in which the individual feels tense and apprehensive that there is some threat. In moderation, it can be useful, but when you are engaging a manipulator on a regular basis, you are likely stuck in a constant cycle of anxious feelings simply due to the manipulator's tactics to keep you in line. Like depressive symptoms, anxious symptoms are no laughing matter and, if pervasive, should be evaluated by a medical professional.

Developing Unhealthy Coping Mechanisms

Sometimes, victims of manipulation develop unhealthy methods of dealing with the stress and anxiety they feel trapped by. They may decide to abuse drugs or alcohol as a way to cope or escape from the feelings of malaise and discomfort that often go along with being a victim of manipulation. The use of drugs or alcohol may allow the individual to stop feeling constant stress as a result of manipulation. It is also possible that the manipulator used drugs or alcohol in order to draw the individual closer, and they quickly spiraled into an addiction that the individual cannot control.

Sometimes, the victims may begin engaging in risky behavior, such as unprotected sex with multiple partners with no regard for the consequences of such actions. They have no concern for having a child or in contracting or spreading an STI and, instead, continue on their self-destructing ways. Sometimes, these behaviors take the form of dangerously speeding down freeways or intentionally going through dangerous areas. Oftentimes, this is because the victim does not care about their own wellbeing, and engaging in these negative, unhealthy coping mechanisms, the individual is able to regain some semblance of control over his or her life.

Sometimes, the unhealthy coping mechanisms are directly self-sabotaging, such as intentionally ruining relationships with other people through aggressive talk with no apologies. Sometimes, the behaviors are harmful, such as eating disorders, both eating too much and refusing to eat, or even self-harm through cutting or burning oneself. These methods all serve as a form of control for the individual, as control is something that is largely lacking from his or her life, to begin with. There is no control of oneself when there are manipulators around because the manipulator will seek to control every aspect of one's life. The manipulator wants control, and because of that, the victim often seeks out other methods to control his or her environment.

Codependency

Codependency refers to a specific pattern of behaviors in which an individual feels entirely dependent upon a relationship for validation and self-worth. The codependent individual sees no point in life without a relationship, and the codependent relationship is the defining factor of the codependent individual. Oftentimes, these people thrive on a feeling of being needed, so they gladly cater to whatever it is a manipulator asks of them. The feeling of being needed is enough for them, at least in the beginning. They are willing to put up with massive amounts of abuse and negative behavior simply because they feel as though they need the relationship and are nothing without it. This is dangerous territory—it leads to the individual feeling as though they absolutely need the manipulator, giving the manipulator another layer of power over the situation at hand. Because the individual feels as though the manipulator is necessary to survive, the manipulator can then threaten to leave any time he or she needs the codependent in line, and it will frequently work.

This behavioral trait is attractive to manipulators simply because they want victims that are easily controlled, and the ones that feel as though life is meaningless without them are not only the biggest ego boosts but also the biggest weapon against the victim. Oftentimes, manipulators will even go out of their way to create a codependent through various emotional manipulation techniques.

Dishonesty

Victims of the abuse and manipulation often endured when involved with a manipulator are inherently ashamed of what is going on. To some degree, they do understand that what is happening is wrong, and yet, they struggle to break free. Instead, they go into denial, convincing themselves that what is happening is acceptable and not nearly as bad as it actually is. They will oftentimes lie to those around them that may question them about what is happening. This is oftentimes magnified by the fact that the victim believes that the manipulation and abuse is his or her own fault and that the entire situation is deserved. They are then doubly ashamed that they are in that mess in the first place while also maintaining a degree of blame that is entirely undeserved.

Lack of Care for Self

Those who have been manipulated frequently stop caring about themselves. They do not take care of themselves first or make themselves a priority because that sort of behavior has been deemed selfish and therefore banned by the manipulator. The individuals feel as though they are being selfish anytime they dare do something for themselves, such as buying a new shirt they liked or investing time or energy into a hobby. They are frequently so broken down that they will go out of their ways to do anything their manipulators request simply because that is what they have been taught to do.

You may notice a friend that no longer engages in hobbies that once consumed his life or a family member who will no longer purchase new clothes, even when hers are beginning to fall apart and need to be replaced. These are examples of ways that the individual being manipulated may stop engaging in self-care. Others may stop working out after being told that they spent too much time at the gym with too many people of the opposite sex and that it made their manipulators uncomfortable. Whatever the change in self-care is, it is incredibly apparent, especially to those around the victim who notice such a change in personality.

Untrusting

After time being manipulated or abused, oftentimes, victims of manipulation are no longer the trusting individuals they once were before. They become so accustomed to being manipulated that they constantly assume that other people have ulterior motives for everything they do. That person that held the door open for her only did so because he wanted a date. The person who smiled and waved only did so because she felt bad for the victim. Of course, both of those statements are likely largely untrue, but the victim of manipulation is in a constant state of anxiety and fearing that there will be manipulation appearing elsewhere in life as well simply because it has been a fact of life for a period of time.

Lack of Self-Esteem

Perhaps one of the most noticeable side effects of manipulation is a massive lack of self-esteem. The best covert manipulators are so skilled at sneaking into the lives of other people and convincing them that they are awful and therefore are beyond blessed to have the manipulator in their lives that they are able to systematically shatter any self-esteem that had been present in the beginning and instead replace it with a feeling of worthlessness. When the victim feels worthless, the victim is not likely to feel as though he or she deserves better treatment, which means that he or she is more likely to stick out any abuse or manipulation for fear of not being able to find a relationship in the future, especially if the manipulator has reiterated just how utterly unlovable an individual is.

Through these techniques, the manipulator systematically demolishes any self-esteem present, and they often seek out those with little self-esteem in the first place. People around the victim may notice the lack of self-esteem but not act upon it, or they may act upon it, and instead of doing something to protect or encourage the victim to leave the relationship, they may push the victim closer to the manipulator. If you notice that a friend or family member suddenly is struggling with self-esteem, it may be worth taking a moment to stop and check in to make sure that the other person is okay. In the best-case scenario, they are perfectly fine but struggling with a rough patch in life. In the worst-case scenario, you may discover that the friend or family member is actually a victim of manipulation or abuse and is in need of extra support to break free.

Chapter 5: Emotional Manipulation Tactics

Emotional manipulation can be absolutely devastating to people. Remember, emotions are massively motivating, and if you manage to manipulate one's emotions properly, you can encourage the individual to cater to your every whim. In doing so, you will be able to get exactly what you want. Of course, these techniques can also be incredibly harmful to the individual they are attempting to control simply because they are putting such a strain on the victim's mental state at the moment.

Understanding Emotions for Manipulation

When using emotional manipulation tactics, the most popular ones play off of one of four emotions: anger, fear, guilt, and sadness. In playing off of these emotions, you are more likely to get the desired results, especially if you understand the implications of each of those emotions. By developing a solid understanding of what each of these emotions entails, you are able to better control people simply by knowing which emotions to trigger.

Anger

Anger can be incredibly motivating. You can use it to direct blame onto someone else or encourage a degrading of a relationship between two people if you are able to trigger it. Remember, anger typically implies a degradation of some important boundary that was violated, and if you understand and recognize the importance of anger, you can wield it to your advantage.

For example, imagine that your victim has a friend that is nosy and seems to be on to the fact that you are manipulating her best friend. You cannot just tell your victim to stop talking to this individual as they are best friends and have been for the better part of a decade. What you can do instead, however, is direct anger toward the best friend to erode at the relationship. You could tell your victim that her friend did or said something harmful about the victim or about yourself in hopes of your victim coming to your defense. Your victim gets angry and directs that anger at the best friend, who, of course, grows defensive, and the entire situation blows up, causing a big argument while you are seen as an innocent bystander to the situation.

Fear

Fear motivates people because it tells them that they are in danger, somehow. This can be incredibly useful to utilize toward people, particularly in situations in which you are responsible for selling something. For example, imagine that you are a real estate agent. You directly get a cut of the value of the house as a commission for facilitating the sale. If your clients have been looking at a house that, admittedly, does fit their needs, but is in a less-than-stellar neighborhood in town and therefore is cheaper than many other similar houses elsewhere, you may mention to the individual that crime has been getting out of control in the area, or that you have heard stories of shootings or finding needles nearby. The entire purpose is to appeal to the fact that the individuals will likely become afraid at the idea of finding needles on their front lawn, and because of that, they are likely to look elsewhere. After all, no one wants to live somewhere; they are afraid to call home.

Guilt

As already discussed, guilt frequently encourages people to meet certain obligations. By appealing to guilt, you are able to tell someone that they have failed in achieving the completion of a specific need, and by accusing the individual of doing so, you are able to convince the other person to give in. For example, if your partner is supposed to take you out to dinner that night at a restaurant that you have had reservations at for the last month but has been seeming hesitant after an unexpected car accident, and deductible wiped out his savings, you may lay on the guilt, reminding him that he promised in an attempt to get him to follow through, though you know that it is not the right thing to do in the circumstances, and may actually put him in a really bad financial spot.

Sadness

Remember, sadness implied that there was a loss or pain somewhere and is meant to remind the individual not to repeat whatever had just happened. It is entirely meant to be discouraging, and it is incredibly powerful. People feel sadness when something significant has happened, but it may also be felt empathetically as well. This is how many charities seek out donations—they show pictures of sad, starving children or animals recovering from surgery needed after they were abused or neglected. In showing these sad images with sad music playing, with a quick message about how you can save the animals or children with a meager daily contribution, these charities are able to encourage people to donate massive amounts of money simply because the people are more willing to do whatever it will take to escape the massive amount of sadness they are feeling as a result of the ad.

Steps to Emotional Manipulation

When engaging in emotional manipulation, then, there are two key steps to follow: you must first create emotions, then exploit them accordingly. In doing these two steps, you will be able to utilize the emotions to encourage whatever it is you feel you need. If you do so properly, you will get the desired results relatively easily.

Remember, fear, guilt, and sadness are the three easiest emotions to manipulate, but anger can be incredibly useful too if you can manage to wield it properly and direct it where it belongs.

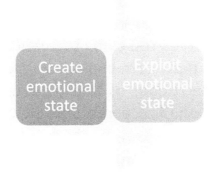

Creating Emotions

Creating emotions is not nearly as difficult as it may sound at first. While it can be tricky to get the hang of, it is not actually that hard. When you understand the process, you are then able to develop intense control over someone. The simplest way to do so is by identifying an individual's triggers. If you understand what it is that triggers the individual, you are able to then ensure that he or she will feel what you want on demand. This can be done by creating connections between certain stimuli and the desired emotions, much like how you can condition people to associate certain stimuli with certain reactions. Usually, however, any conditioning you are doing should be a bit more covert and go unnoticed wherever possible. After all, you do not want your victim to understand what you are doing, or you risk ruining the entire process.

A good way to start emotions is to create emotional triggers yourself. Start by telling a sad story, for example, and as you are doing so, engage in something subtle and repetitive. You could tap your arm in a specific pattern or touch the victim in a specific way. Do this over time, repeating a trigger of that particular emotion you are attempting to utilize and a specific touch or tapping pattern. Over time, your victim will unconsciously associate your touch or tapping pattern with the feeling of sadness, guilt, anger, or whatever else you were attempting to establish through the process.

Exploiting Emotions

With the triggers identified or created, you are then able to exploit them. This is when you are able to actually get whatever it is that you are seeking out. If your partner, for example, tells you no, he cannot take you out to dinner. You can nod your head but simultaneously touch your partner in the way you have associated with guilt. You tell him you are disappointed, but you understand in a sad voice and touch his arm, patting it. He feels guilty even though he may have had legitimate reasons to cancel on you, and he then decides that the guilt is too much and makes it up to you, either at that restaurant or at another one that is more affordable. Of course, there are several other methods you can use beyond that pattern of creating emotion and then exploiting it that are also considered forms of emotional manipulation.

Gaslighting

Gaslighting is another form of emotional manipulation in which the goal is to create a feeling of apprehension and self-doubt. If you are gaslighting someone, you essentially deny his or her perception of reality around you, convincing the other party that he or she is wrong and reiterating your perception instead. Of course, your perception is likely wrong or exaggerated to serve your point diligently. This is done through various steps of denying the perception of the individual you are gaslighting with increasing intensity until you can deny that the house is painted blue and the individual is likely to believe you.

Of course, this is dangerous—you are literally telling someone that their perception of reality is wrong and that they cannot trust themselves. You are teaching the other person that he or she may very well be losing his or her mind, and, in the process, you are convincing him or her to be reliant on your own perceptions, making a more vulnerable, more complacent victim. After all, all you will have to do is quietly remind your victim how he always seems to have trouble understanding what is happening, and the victim will immediately defer to your judgment.

When you are attempting to gaslight someone, you first start small. Deny something relatively unimportant. For example, ask your victim where he left his car keys so you can go get your jacket you forgot out of his car. He may tell you they are hanging up on the key rack. You go get them and run outside. When you come back, you tell him that the keys were actually on the kitchen counter. This is small and harmless, but it begins to build up self-doubt. You slowly continue to implement these sorts of denials of the individual's perceptions, sometimes using the amount of some food costs, or denying the day of the week last week, they went out with friends. Slowly, you begin to ramp it up, using larger examples. You may convince him that his doctor's appointment is on Tuesday when it is on Wednesday, and then when he calls you out, you tell him you know it was Wednesday; you have been insisting it was Wednesday for weeks, and *he* kept saying Tuesday, not you. You can deny saying things in a conversation that you are actively having, or deny that a certain show was on the night prior, despite the fact that he is certain it was. Eventually, he will be unsure he understands reality at all, and you will be free to control him.

Love Bombing and Devaluing

Love bombing and devaluing create a wicked cycle in which you put your victim on a pedestal, showering him or her in love before promptly pushing him or her off of said pedestal and making the victim vie for your approval to get elevated once more. It involves two key stages: Love bombing and devaluing, as you likely gathered from the name. Each stage is crucial to getting the desired effect.

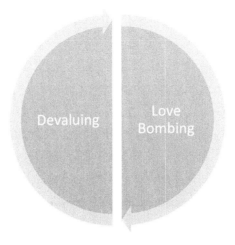

First, you begin by love bombing. This stage has one important purpose: Making the other person addicted to you. You may shower her in praises and affection, making it clear to her that you feel you are the luckiest person in the world to have someone like her around you. You tell her how much you care and constantly take her out on dates. You push the relationship to move quickly, making it into a whirlwind romance, and you constantly shower her with gifts that are not quite appropriate for the amount of time you have been together but insist that she takes them. When you feel that she is sufficiently hooked, essentially creating an addiction to the rush of endorphins she gets every time you look at her after building her up and placing her atop of the pedestal; you move on to devaluing.

When you devalue her, you want to make her feel as low as possible. You tell her that she does not matter to you, that she is lucky you so much as looked at her, and that she does not deserve anything. You want to make her miserable and confused, unsure why you suddenly stopped loving her after such an intense period of time. She becomes desperate to get back to that place of romance and love on a pedestal and is willing to do whatever it takes to get back. If you do this skillfully, you are able to play with her emotions to the point that she understands that displeasing you will result in devaluation, which makes her constantly interested in ensuring that you are happy within the relationship.

Silent Treatment

When you engage in the silent treatment, you are not just taking a break to calm yourself—you are systematically refusing to engage with the victim simply to voice your displeasure with your silence. You refuse to acknowledge that the victim exists at all, and in doing so, you make it clear that you are unhappy. Humans naturally crave love and acceptance as social creatures. We want to be acknowledged, especially by those we love, and manipulators know this. You want to use that knowledge to your advantage, similarly to in the love bombing and devaluing technique. You become so enraged with your partner that instead of engaging with him or her, you stop speaking. You know that it hurts your partner or victim, and you can see that you are hurting the other person, but you continue anyway. The entire purpose is to punish, and if the victim looks hurt, then you have successfully utilized the silent treatment.

It is important to note that while the silent treatment may get the other person desperate to engage with you, it is not healthy to use in a relationship. If you are legitimately attempting a relationship with someone who you legitimately love and want to be happy, the silent treatment is one of the quickest ways to sour and destroy the relationship altogether. It breeds contempt and resentment, which can quickly culminate in the destruction of the relationship entirely. Remember, manipulation has no place in a relationship, but the silent treatment can become particularly dangerous to utilize if you have little regard for how the other person will respond to it.

Aggression or Anger

Sometimes, the easiest way to convince the other person to do what it is that you want or need is through more coercive means. You need to scare the victim in order to get obedience through fear, or at least, you assume you need to. When you want to convince people to be obedient, you may see value in utilizing intimidation or subtle threats. You know that they lead to discomfort in the victim, and that is exactly why you do so. You know that the discomfort will lead to the other person caving and not bothering to push the point further.

Utilizing your aggression or anger can take several different forms. You can threaten action or imply threats, such as saying that your partner will not like you if you are pushed, or you may even decide to do things that border on illegal but never quite cross the line into assault and battery, such as punching holes in the wall or attempting to otherwise make your partner fear your reaction.

You may even resort to tantrums in general, screaming and crying when you do not get your way, knowing that the other person is not likely to challenge you if you put on this largely angry show. Of course, you will likely have to slowly escalate this as the victim becomes accustomed to your behaviors over time.

Passive Aggressive Communication

Sometimes, you may decide that you will resort to passive-aggressive comments to get your point across. You may say things that are just snide enough to be offensive but are ambiguous enough that they can be plausibly denied, such as the example provided earlier with the salad comment. You may employ the help of a friend or family member to talk to your partner and mention just how unhappy you are. You may even decide to engage in behaviors that are directly contradictory to what you have said, making it clear that you disapprove.

For example, if your partner has apologized for not finishing up yard work on time and promises to do it that night, you may agree, but then as soon as he shows up at home, you leave him home alone with three young children so getting the time necessary to complete the project becomes an impossibility. He cannot possibly get out on time to mow the lawn when you are not home, and your young children are home with him—it would not be safe to either have them outside while he mowed or left indoors without anyone to watch them.

Chapter 6: Influence Without Manipulation

Of course, not all social influence has to be manipulative either. There are several different ways that you can engage in influencing other people without ever having to step into the realm of manipulation if you would prefer to avoid it. These methods are largely more ethical and are meant to be beneficial to the other person as well, so you are not only taking advantage of another person for your own benefit.

Influence can be particularly useful in situations that are not suitable for manipulation or when manipulation would likely violate any contracts or job descriptions you have at that point in time. Overall, you can think of many of the persuasive methods that will be discussed here as the ethical, work-appropriate techniques that can be used without losing a license to practice medicine, sell a product, or practice law.

Principles of Persuasion

The principles of persuasion refer to a set of six different techniques that people find inherently persuasive. In using these principles of persuasion, you are able to convince people to do things legitimately and honestly simply by appealing to one of six different principles. Of course, using any of these is not a guarantee for success, but rather it ups your chances of naturally convincing the other person to do whatever it is you are requesting of them. The six principles of persuasion are reciprocity, likability, authority, social proof, scarcity, and consistency, and commitment.

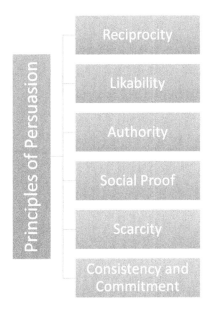

Reciprocity

Reciprocity refers to the idea that people naturally want to return favors after they have had one done for them. Think of the feeling of obligation you may get when someone gives you a birthday present—you feel the need to return the favor when the other person's birthday rolls around. This is for a specific reason: you are convinced through reciprocity. This is sort of nature's failsafe to the selfless behavior that humans have developed throughout evolution: With reciprocity, humans feel the need to return the favor whenever anyone helps them in any way.

Good, strong leaders recognize reciprocity as an inherent way the human mind works, and they will frequently bank on it—this is why you will see people ask, "What can I do for you?" when you come in somewhere. They are making it clear that they are interested in helping you, and hopefully, in return, you will help them as well. Good, emotionally intelligent leaders will almost always ask what they can do to help someone else before they ever ask the favor they had in mind. You can do this as well—offer to do something for someone. They will think that you are doing so out of the goodness of your heart. You may be, at least in part, but you will still have an ulterior motive. You can then ask the other person for a favor when you need it. For example, if you need to have your shift changed for a concert you really want to attend in two months, you may volunteer the next time one of your coworkers mentions needing time off and needing a shift covered to get it approved. Your coworker then will probably offer to do something if he can repay you, at which point you can mention that you actually need your shift covered for the concert you want to go to, and your coworker agrees to do so. Now, you are left satisfied because your shift is covered, and you were not required to use manipulation to make it happen.

Likability

Likability refers to the fact that people naturally are more inclined to be persuaded when they like the person doing the persuading. After all, would you rather do a favor for your spouse, who you presumably love, or that coworker that you cannot stand? The answer is almost definitely that you would rather do something for your spouse, and the biggest reason for that is because you actually like your spouse.

Studies have shown that people are more likely to reach agreements in negotiations when all members take a moment to introduce themselves with some small tidbit of information about themselves that makes them more relatable. The biggest reason for this is due to the fact that they become relatable, and when you relate to someone, you are more likely to want to come up with a compromise with them because you are more likely to feel empathetic toward them.

Luckily, there are three surefire ways to establish yourself as likable, even if your interaction with someone is relatively short. In fact, you will only need to take a few moments to do three simple things. You must first make yourself relatable, such as offering a small detail about yourself into the conversation naturally. Next, you should offer some sort of legitimate compliment to the other person. Lastly, you need to establish yourself as willing to cooperate in order to reach the same goal, effectively creating a team mentality. These three things can be the difference between landing that sale at work or failing to close.

Authority

People most often are willing to respect authority. They are usually willing to listen to someone who has established himself as an authority, and for that reason, those viewed as authority figures are typically seen as more persuasive than those who are not. After all, you are more likely to listen to your dentist about how to save that tooth than the random cashier at the grocery store. This is due to your inherent bias that the dentist is more knowledgeable about dentistry than the cashier, and you are likely right, though it is possible (and highly unlikely) that your cashier did, in fact, go to school for dentistry.

When you want to make yourself an authority, you want to make it clear that you know what you are talking about. You can do so by displaying your diplomas and other licenses you may have acquired during your career in your office. You can display awards that show just how good at your job you are. You could try including your credentials on your name placard on your desk or nametag. You could even have a secretary whose job is to sing your praises when answering the phone or greeting prospective clients. If all of that is impractical with your job, there are other methods you can utilize as well—you can drop hints toward your experience in whatever topic you are discussing in a way that is natural with the client, such as mentioning that when you studied business back in graduate school, you learned certain concepts relevant to the conversation you are having. Simply dropping your experience in conversation makes it clearer that you do, in fact, have some sort of experience, and therefore, your judgment should be trusted.

Social Proof

Social proof refers to the fact that people largely are more influenced by their peers than through simply being told what to do for no real reason. This is essentially utilizing peer pressure in order to control someone else, or recognizing that the principles of peer pressure are relevant to social interactions. For example, people are more likely to go along with the behaviors of their peers that they relate to when they feel out of their element.

This can absolutely be used in manipulation and persuasion—you can hint that other people in a similar position made a choice similar to whatever you want the other person to do. For example, if you want to sell a mother of three children a car, you may point out that many of the parents that you sell to in the same boat as the mother oftentimes buy a minivan or SUV for the extra space for supplies for sports and extracurricular activities or even just to make up for the fact that children grow and may even outgrow a smaller car, feeling completely cramped if they do not have a third row to spread back toward. The mother may feel pressured as you mention this and be a bit more inclined to defer to what other people doing simply because she was unsure anyway, and if other people are doing it, it likely works well.

Scarcity

The principle of scarcity is little more than supply and demand—people think that things that are scarce are more valuable simply because they are not as easily attained. With that in mind, you can absolutely make something seem more desirable or valuable simply by creating an artificial scarcity of the item. Companies do this frequently—you will see companies with business models that surround selling seasonal or limited time only items and they draw out massive amounts of attention simply because everyone wants to get their hands on that new limited edition item, or they have been dying for that seasonal drink for months now, and they are absolutely thrilled that it is finally available again.

When you want to use scarcity to control someone else, you can do so simply by making yourself scarce. Particularly in relationships, you see this utilized in one partner threatening to break up with the other, making it clear that their presence and commitment to the relationship is not, in fact, guaranteed, and if the other person cannot figure out what they are doing, then the person creating the ultimatum is willing to walk away altogether.

Consistency and Commitment

The last of the principles of persuasion is consistency and commitment. This refers to the fact that humans naturally value consistency, and the easiest way to get that consistency is through commitments that are meant to motivate the individual to go through with what was committed to simply to become consistent. For example, someone who has committed to do something for you is likely going to follow through because with commitment comes obligation, and failing at obligations begets guilt, which most people want to avoid. If you want someone to do something, then you must first start with a commitment to something small. It does not have to be particularly significant—even asking to borrow a pen would start this process. When that first commitment has been made, then the individual is already in the mindset to continue saying yes, enabling you to continue asking for whatever it is that you need. You can then attempt to get the other person to do something else, and you are somewhat more likely to get them to agree if you have already asked them to do something that they agreed to do.

Ethos, Pathos, Logos

Alongside the principles of persuasion, there is also the theory of ethos, pathos, and logos—three Greek words meant to refer to appeals to different aspects of life to convince other people. When using these, you are essentially creating arguments in which you convince or compel someone to agree to do something because your argument is simply too compelling to deny.

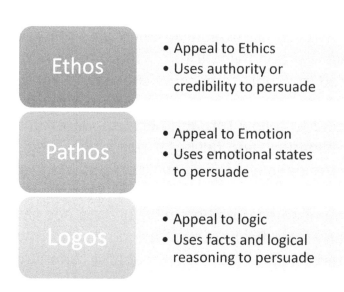

Ethos

Ethos means ethics—it refers to appeals to ethical or moral duties. When you make an argument rooted in ethos, you are arguing for ethics. You are making it a point to spell out exactly why it is so important to do things a certain way in order to avoid violating any of those inherent values of right vs. wrong.

Ethos can also be used in another method than simply appealing to one's own moral code—it can be used to argue that an authority figure has said that things should be a certain way, and therefore should be followed. You see this oftentimes in advertisements—a commercial will employ a well-known figure to advocate for a product in hopes of other people naturally following along simply because they know of the other person and respect that particular person's judgment.

You could utilize ethos yourself by telling the person you are attempting to persuade about how doing what it is you are requesting is morally expected or required. For example, if you are attempting to collect donations for a charity, you could tell the other person that it is morally superior to donate whatever you can and that the goodness in your heart is ultimately what matters at the end of the day.

Pathos

Pathos, in contrast, is an appeal to emotions. When you are using pathos, you are directly creating an emotional response. Think of this as being what those commercials begging for donations for the poor children in Africa or the money to take care of the abused kittens with the sad eyes use in order to convince you to give. When you use pathos, you are directly trying to convince the target audience to do something because their emotions tell them they should.

Logos

Lastly, logos refers to an appeal to logic. When you are utilizing logos, you are offering up cold, hard facts and numbers in an attempt to appeal to the other person's ability to reason about what is happening. The entire point is to create a cohesive, logical argument that does not hinge upon an authority figure or an emotional state. In appealing to logos, you are able to create a largely foolproof argument that is more difficult to take down with objections unless the information utilized was falsified to begin with. For example, if you are trying to get someone to invest in your company, you may provide a figure for the average return on investment from the last few years.

Neuro-Linguistic Programming

Neuro-linguistic programming is an approach to psychology involving strategies that enable an individual to understand how people's minds work, and in knowing how their minds work, is then able to alter the behaviors of that person. Most often, it is intended to be used for people who are actively desiring a change in their behaviors, but it can be used to influence and persuade people without their knowledge as well. This is done through three key factors—the brain's language and understanding how to change behaviors by speaking the language of the brain.

Essentially, NLP assumes that the brain functions in a way that it understands and has its own language (let's say French for the purpose of this example). Your body, however, speaks English. When your body tells your brain something, it oftentimes gets lost in translation, and the end result is getting something that was undesired. This is because your body and mind cannot quite communicate because they are speaking different languages that are unintelligible to each other. However, NLP believes that you can actually change your own behaviors by using methods that the brain does understand.

Most often, in the context of influence and persuasion, people use mirroring and anchoring.

Mirroring

Mirroring is one of the most fundamental skills you can develop through NLP. It refers to the ability to mimic back what someone else is doing in order to develop rapport, which allows you to be more persuasive in general. This technique basically enables you to make yourself likable in a short period of time, which then gives you the credibility needed to make your points persuasively.

When you are mirroring, you are first developing the connection and then acting upon it. There are several steps to this process, including:

- **Foster minor connection:** The first step is creating a minor connection, so the rest of your attempts are well-received. In order to do this, start by facing forward. You want to make sure that your body is oriented in a way that you are actively listening and making eye contact. Do three subtle nods in order to encourage the other person to continue speaking—it gives the perception that you agree with the other person. Then convince yourself that this person is, in fact, interesting to you.

- **Mimic vocal cues:** With a minor connection developed, you then should make it a point to match the vocal cues the other person is using. In particular, you should focus on the speed and pitch of the other person. In doing so, you are able to convince them that you are both invested the same amount to the topic at hand.

- **The punctuator:** Your next step is to identify the punctuator, which is something that the other person is using exclusively for emphasis. It could be a specific hand movement or something like a tilt of the head, a specific expression, or even raising of the eyebrows in a certain way. Figure out what it is, and the next time you are certain the other person is getting ready to use a punctuator, make sure you do it as well. It fosters a more intimate connection between the two of you.

- **Test:** Lastly, make sure the connection is, in fact, there. You can do so by making a small movement that feels natural in the conversation. Try scratching your nose or rubbing your hands together. If you are across the table from each other, you can also try taking a drink. If the other person seems to follow your lead, mimicking exactly what you have done, you likely have developed a decent amount of rapport and connection.

Anchoring

Anchoring refers to the process through which you take one bad habit that you wish to change somehow, and you essentially anchor a good habit in its place. You do this by first identifying the bad habit that needs to be changed. Perhaps you want to change your friend's tendency to contradict you constantly. In this case, you may know that your friend has a tendency to contradict you when your friend is feeling annoyed about something. What you would want to do, then, is change your friend's tendency from being annoyed leading to contradictions to your friend being annoyed leading to something more productive.

You can do this by identifying what it is that annoys him in the first place. Perhaps he gets annoyed when his favorite football team loses. Unfortunately, he likes a team that loses a lot, so you spend the entirety of football season miserable and wishing he would change his behaviors. What you would do, then, is ensure that you do something pleasant every time his favorite team loses. Perhaps you decide that you take him out to tacos every time the team loses. He then starts to associate losing with tacos, and eventually, instead of getting angry and combative when his team loses, he prioritizes going out for tacos for the group instead. Now, you no longer deal with the annoying contradictions and combative attitude, and your friend is completely unaware that you essentially reprogrammed his connections between his team losing and tacos.

Chapter 7: Manipulation in Relationships

Relationships, by and large, are supposed to be commitments between two people to create them. They involve free will, respect, communication, commitment, and compromise. However, when manipulation gets introduced to the scene, a lot of that all falls apart. It becomes difficult to have a relationship when manipulation blows away nearly every defining aspect of the relationship. When relationships are meant to be healthy, there is no room for toxic manipulation.

After all, look at the definition of manipulation again as a refresher—it is meant to be an influence that is created through insidious, covert, and likely exploitative motivation behind it. You cannot be in a legitimate relationship with someone that you are attempting to manipulate and coerce into obedience; that is no longer a relationship built upon communication, commitment, and compromise. In fact, there are none of those things—when you manipulate within a relationship; you essentially create a situation in which communication is slim-to-none—you do not care to listen; all you want is obedience. There is no commitment; only obedience, and respect to you while your partner is not allowed to make decisions of his or her own free will. There is no compromise because the manipulator makes all of the decisions and does not listen, nor care about the victim's desires.

It is, however, important to note that there is a difference between the social influence that happens naturally and healthily within relationships and the influence of manipulation—relationships do, in fact, have a basis in influence, but not in coercive influence. In a healthy relationship, relationships are meant to bring out the best in each other. Both parties in the relationship learn and adopt new skills and desires, and in response, both parties also develop and grow. One member may realize that he actually really likes certain foods, while the other never realized how fun video games could be. That sort of change is not manipulation but rather is a social influence that occurred organically and therefore is healthy. After all, people do grow, and their tastes do change over time.

There are several signs and effects that become apparent when a relationship is largely manipulative or one-sided. In these instances, these relationships are meant not to better both parties, but only one. One person holds all of the power while the other is forced to repeatedly give without ever receiving in return. Of course, it is incredibly difficult to identify whether your relationship is legitimately manipulative or if you are too sensitive, especially if the other party is the one being manipulative. However, you should still familiarize yourself with what to expect within a manipulative relationship just in case the information ever becomes relevant to you.

Signs of a Manipulative Relationship

There are several signs that your relationship may have developed unhealthily and needs some work. Please keep in mind that manipulation does not have to be a part of your life if you are the victim. If you are the manipulator, recognize the fact that your relationships are not going to work out if your entire purpose is to manipulate and control the other party; you are not looking for a relationship if you are looking for control, you are looking for a slave or an employee. Nevertheless, there are 10 signs there is a manipulator within your relationship.

Accusations

Oftentimes, accusations rear their heads in a relationship involving a manipulator. The victim often feels the need to call out the manipulator, especially in the early days, when the behaviors are only just then beginning to escalate. From there, the manipulator feels the need to defend him or herself, taking on a victim persona and attempting to gaslight the victim into believing it is the victim's fault.

Mind Games

Mind games happen constantly in the relationship when a manipulator is present. Oftentimes, the manipulator wants to ensure that the victim feels insecure and uncomfortable in the relationship with the sole purpose of making the victim easier to control. People are usually more easily persuaded and controlled when they are feeling upset, sad, fearful, or guilty, and the manipulator seeks to accomplish exactly that.

Things Are Constantly Damaged

The manipulator may pretend it is an accident, but frequently intentionally damages the belongings of the victim. This is done again to make the victim more easily maintained due to feeling upset about the loss of something important. The manipulator absolutely knew just how important that item was, but chose to damage it anyway out of spite.

Jealousy

Oftentimes, the manipulator in a relationship will foster jealousy in the victim as a carte blanche to do whatever he or she wants. This is because any time that the victim voices a complaint, the manipulator can simply say the victim is being jealous and needs to get over it, enabling the manipulator to be able to flirt or even cheat on the victim without the victim being able to make an argument against it.

Always a Victim

Remember, the manipulator frequently will take on a victim role simply to avoid blame and will make it a point to somehow direct blame toward the real victim instead. In being an expert at blaming the other party, they are quite convincing, leaving the victim beginning to believe the story. Fearing that he or she is the manipulator or abuse, the true victim oftentimes gets caught in a loop of being even more easily manipulated out of fear of being manipulative or abusive by resisting.

Guilt

The manipulator will always wield guilt because it is so effective. The best manipulators are able to make anything the victim's fault. Did your ex-husband forget to pick up your children for his custody time at school? That is your fault because you did not remind him, even though you are not his keeper. Did the pizza burn? It is because you did not get up and check it when you should have since you know how to cook well and should have known better.

Rushed into Decisions

The manipulator will frequently rush the victim into decisions, constantly wanting decisions immediately. There is never any allowance for considering something seriously, and the manipulator wants everything to be done in snap decisions. This is to get what they want, knowing that what they want may seem like a good idea at the time.

Inconsistency Between Actions and Words

Frequently, the manipulator will say one thing but do the exact opposite. They use their words to get what they want, frequently telling people that they will change or do better just to get the complacency that they desire, only to revert right back to their old ways after the fact. If they do happen to break a promise and revert back to old mentalities, it will, of course, be the fault of the victim and not the manipulator.

Constant Negotiation

Within the relationship, the manipulator will make the victim believe that he or she is getting concessions when, in fact, the only one benefitting is the manipulator. Of course, the manipulator will attempt to make it seem like the victim also stood to gain something, even if that gain is nonexistent or a figment of the manipulator's imagination.

Words Are Constantly Distorted

Lastly, manipulators are constantly spinning words and taking them out of context. A good emotional manipulator is able to take something that the victim has said and spin it around to mean the exact opposite of what it meant and even convince the victim of the intention, leaving the victim confused by the entire process.

Effects of a Manipulative Relationship

At the end of the day, a relationship with an individual firmly rooted in manipulation is entirely unhealthy. The individual being manipulated is going to suffer immensely; the longer the relationship goes on. The victim is at an increased risk of mental and physical health issues that can be completely debilitating, and when the individual is suffering, there is no way that he or she is actually a healthy, productive member of the relationship. With the problems provided, the individual is crushed, kept unloved and unwanted in the relationship with no real recourse. It becomes difficult to leave the manipulative relationship because the victim can hardly tell up from down, let alone navigate ending a relationship. It becomes even more complicated if children were an active part of the relationship as well, as then the victim is looking at a court battle with a manipulator that can likely drag out the court case for years.

The manipulator is also likely to drag the victim back into the relationship every time he or she attempts to leave, and unfortunately, the manipulator knows exactly how best to appeal to the victim, enabling his or her success relatively easily. The end result is a strange corruption of a legitimate relationship, in which both parties of the relationship fail to better the other, and in fact, both parties bring out the worst in each other. The victim brings out the manipulator, through no fault of his or her own, and the manipulator brings out the worst, most broken self in the victim.

Chapter 8: Manipulation in the Workplace

Do you have a coworker that everyone avoids? Perhaps you are frequently attempting to avoid discussing anything of value around that particular person out of fear for it coming back to haunt you in the future. Any time that coworker draws near, a hush may fall over the group in an attempt to avoid spilling any of the important beans that could potentially hurt any of you. You all knew he was trouble, but none of you could get rid of him. His methods were too sneaky, and while everyone knew not to trust him, he was protected by the union, and everyone was forced to put up with him, despite everyone clearly being unhappy about it in the first place.

Did that description pull up a picture in your mind of someone in particular? If it did, that is a major red flag— you may have a manipulator in the workplace. Workplace manipulators are just as dangerous as romantic manipulators that work within romantic relationships. In fact, they can actually be worse in many ways because your livelihood depends on your ability to continue to put up with the manipulator despite the fact that you do not want to. You have no choice but to stick things out and hope that it does not get bad enough to drive you to quit and that you do not get the angry eye of the manipulator fixed on making your life as miserable as possible.

Signs of Workplace Manipulation

No matter how miserable the workplace maybe, you feel as though you are stuck. You may love your job but hate the people—all you know is that every time you walk into your workplace, you feel a sense of despair or dread settle over you. If you suspect that you may be being manipulated, it is time to consider the possibility that someone in your office is a detriment. This section will provide you with five signs that there is a manipulator somewhere within your workplace.

You Feel Upset, Sad, or Depressed Around Someone

This may not be immediately noticeable to you, but you may be able to pick up the pattern. If you are often upset or uncomfortable at work, try to stop and notice whoever is around you every time it happens. The fact that you are feeling uneasy already implies that there is something going on outside of your control, and you should pay attention to that. Remember that you have your gut instinct for a reason and respect it.

Look around when you start to feel stressed and make a mental note of every person around. Make it a point to look around when you realize that you are feeling at ease as well. Ultimately, you are likely to feel stressed out and uncomfortable around the manipulator in your life, and the best way to recognize the manipulator when you are unsure who it could possibly be is to check on who is around when you are and are not comfortable. Take note—it may surprise you.

You Feel a Sense of Obligation to Someone

Yet again, obligation has made a return. However, it is an incredibly effective predictor of manipulation. While some obligation is natural, such as toward your friends and family members, it is not normal to feel an unexplainable amount of obligation toward a coworker for no reason that you can identify.

Oftentimes, in the workplace, obligation takes the form of being asked to do a favor that bothers you after the other person had helped you out when you were in a tight spot. Even though you feel like you would rather forego the favor altogether, you feel as though you have no choice but to go along with it. You know that if you do not go through with it, there will be a problem that you would much rather avoid at all costs. This can be dangerous at work—it makes it, so people feel that they are not able to do what they need to at work when they constantly feel like their obligation is holding them back somehow. They eventually feel as though they cannot make decisions that would be responsible or smart out of fear of making it too tough to follow through with past obligations that they would rather not be dealing with it in the first place anyway.

You Have Changed

Yes, people do change naturally as they grow, and there are ways that a workplace can naturally and healthily change an individual. However, if you feel as though you have changed how you behave at work, or even some of the values you have always upheld simply because of a person at work in the hopes of getting along or avoiding conflict, you have a problem. This is toxic—you should never feel like you have to sacrifice yourself and your values for someone else. Doing so only causes you problems and encourages a toxic workplace environment to further develop.

You Find Someone in the Office Unpredictable

Manipulators are very quick to shift from one emotion or reaction to the other at the drop of a hat. They may be perfectly happy as they speak to you kindly, but as soon as they look at someone else, their entire demeanor can change as they engage in passive-aggressive insults toward someone who had irritated them earlier in the day, and you find yourself suddenly shocked at the change. You did not expect such a personality shift, and for a good reason—those kinds of shifts are unhealthy. People usually have a certain level of stability about them that keeps them from behaving erratically or emotionally in the way that the manipulator does.

Of course, the manipulator has ulterior motives for these behaviors and is attempting to get those around him or her to follow blindly.

You Feel Devalued

No matter how hard you work around the manipulator, however, you find yourself being insulted and devalued. You can try endlessly, and yet the individual still dislikes you. He will still insult you. He will still tell you that your opinion is stupid or worthless. In the end, although you are required to be at work and participate, the manipulator makes it clear that everyone around is so clueless at keeping the workplace flowing that the manipulator is the one running the job, and that is fine with him. He will gladly run the show so long as everyone else follows you.

The manipulator may not even have to say anything to you to make his disapproval clear. Even a dirty look could be enough to send chills down your spine and leave you feeling unhappy and embarrassed. Nevertheless, you still make it a point to try to behave in ways that make the manipulator happy, though you know that there is little reason or benefit to doing so.

Effect of Workplace Manipulation

Ultimately, the impact of workplace manipulation is horrible—the employees are left miserable. If the boss is the manipulator, the employees constantly feel as though nothing they do is good enough, and that is a huge morale killer. Without the necessary morale, individuals likely find themselves miserable and wishing for more stability in the workplace. They have no choice but to put up with abusive tendencies, their own feelings of guilt and insecurity, and failure to generally manage a functional business.

Businesses run by manipulators or manipulators in the office typically create an entirely toxic environment. Despite the fact that they may try their best to cover up the toxicity behind productivity and showing that their largely manipulative methods must have been at least somewhat effective, the manipulators are still managing to spread their toxicity. The people grow restless and less invested in the environment in general. Toxicity makes it, so people slowly grow less productive. Relationships in the workplace fail. The team mentality that so many companies emphasize and push falls apart.

Ultimately, the only way to stop this workplace manipulation is by cutting it out altogether. The most effective way to keep the workplace healthy would be through ensuring that the toxicity does not make it into the workplace, to begin with, but that does not necessarily work when the toxicity has already spread. In those instances, your best bet is to ensure that you come to develop realistic expectations. Expect the individual to be manipulative and assume that he or she will continue to attempt to demean you. Nevertheless, you can persevere through it and use some of the techniques that you will be introduced to shortly to protect yourself, or you can attempt finding a new job altogether. If that is not an option, you could also attempt to bring up the manipulation during an HR meeting or with a supervisor. By and large, most people do not want to put up with workplace manipulators, and if you can combat one, you will likely be able to purify the environment, given enough time.

Chapter 9: How to Eliminate Manipulative People

If you have, in fact, found yourself suffering from emotional manipulation, know that you do not have to put up with it. You can, in fact, decide to change your perception of the relationship you are in and leave if you desire to do so. In fact, leaving is likely for the best, as you will be able to heal as an individual from all of the damage the manipulator has likely done. Know that manipulators are masters at persuading other people, and while the manipulator in your life may be attempting to convince you that you are crazy or overreacting, recognize that you are not. You deserve to live free from the abuse of manipulation. You deserve to have your own free will. You deserve to be entirely happy.

Luckily, there are ways that you can achieve this happiness and ensure that you get the life you deserve. This chapter will guide you through seven tips to directly counter the manipulation attempts you may find yourself facing, and in countering them, you can better protect yourself in the future. Please remember that it is okay to decide you are done in a relationship or workplace with a manipulator, and there is no reason for you to put up with it once you know it is there, and you are ready to leave.

Know the Signs

The most important way you can eliminate manipulation in your life is to make sure you are aware of the signs. Congratulations! By reading through this book, you can check that off of the list. Remember, the methods that manipulators use are oftentimes incredibly insidious and are meant to be harmful. The manipulator wants you to give in and do whatever the manipulator wants without you realizing that you are being manipulated in the first place. However, if you know the signs, you can notice when a red flag goes up, and when that flag does, in fact, fly, you are able to act. If you notice that the manipulator is attempting to coerce you or guilt you, if you are aware that those are techniques manipulators favor, you are able to then avoid falling for it simply because you know it is there. Knowing the warning signs is your first defense against manipulation.

Be Assertive

Remember, the manipulator is counting on your remaining cooperative. In fact, you were likely selected to be manipulated because you are not combative in general. However, that complacency, that desire to remain silent and put up with the manipulation, does not have to define you any longer. If you are able to stop and become assertive about your wants and needs, the manipulator may decide you are no longer worthwhile. For example, if you know what you want to get a chance to pick out a restaurant once and a while on a date night, assert that and refuse to back down. If you want to make sure you are no longer called names or told you are worthless, assert that, and refuse to back down.

This can be a particularly difficult skill to master, but you can do it. There are seven key points to remember when being assertive, and if you can do so, you will be able to make your points clearly and concisely, though the manipulator will likely try to find some way to spin things to be your own fault. These are the seven steps to becoming a more assertive, and therefore less easily manipulated individual:

- **Make sure you are clear:** The most important thing when being assertive is ensuring you express yourself clearly. Use direct, clear, and calm language.

- **Maintain eye contact:** As you assert yourself, make sure you face the individual and make eye contact as you do. This shows that you are not willing to back down.

- **Open, positive posture:** Remember, there is a difference between assertive and aggressive—you are aiming for assertive here. Make sure that you are upright, relaxed, and facing the other person. Make sure your arms are not crossed, and your jaw is not tense. You do not want to come across as aggressive or unwilling to communicate.

- **Plan your point in advance:** Make sure you have a general plan for what you are asserting. Back it up with facts, if necessary. This keeps you from getting flustered, which can quickly become defensive and negative.

- **Do not be afraid to call a time out:** If you need it, it is okay to take a time out from the situation. If emotions begin to run to high, you are well within your rights to call for a break to regather your thoughts and recollect yourself before continuing.

- **Avoid any attacks or accusations:** Make sure your language is as non-aggressive as possible. Statements should always begin with "I" instead of "You" in order to avoid confrontational language. Instead of saying, "You hurt my feelings," you would word it as, "I'm feeling bad."

- **Remain calm:** When you are asserting yourself, ensure that you do manage to keep yourself calm and under control. Doing so ensures that you cannot be made the aggressor in the argument. It also makes sure the manipulator cannot attempt to manipulate your emotions in order to get a rise out of you.

Avoid Suspected Manipulators

Ultimately, the most effective way to escape the grasp of a manipulator is by separating yourself from manipulators altogether. You cannot be manipulated if you have no contact with the manipulator, after all. For this reason, if you suspect that someone in your general vicinity is a manipulator, you should probably make it a point to end the relationship or keep your space. Of course, a manipulator who has targeted you is going to do one of two things in this instance: Pursue you more, or let you go because you have proven that you are not an easy target. After all, most manipulators would prefer an easy target over one who is going to constantly put up a fight.

Never Give Up Values

Manipulators always want to force you to give. However, no matter how much a manipulator guilts you, you should have a set of values that you refuse to back down on. These values are likely your innermost beliefs; they could be religious or moral in nature, and they likely define your own behaviors. Do not let the manipulator erode at those values. In making it clear that you will stick to your convictions and refuse to back down, you are telling the manipulator that there is no way you are willing to give in. You ensure that you are honoring values and beliefs in a way that you will never give up on, and the manipulator has to either accept that or move on to someone else that will give up on those beliefs.

Always Take Time to Consider Options

No matter how much the manipulator may try to pressure you into making a decision right at that moment, remember that it is entirely acceptable to push off most major decisions a day. For example, if the manipulator wants you to take out a car loan for him or her and is pressuring you to do so that night, you are well within your rights to stop, tell the manipulator that you would prefer to take the night to consider it, and actually follow through with weighing the pros and cons. After all, something like that is a major purchase that will take years to pay off, and you will be responsible for the car if the manipulator does anything or decides to no longer pay for it.

While the manipulator may wish that you would be willing to give in right that second, remember that you can make these decisions for yourself. You need to make decisions that are right for you, even if you are married to the manipulator in the example. All major decisions should always be slept on and considered before they are impulsively followed. After all, something that seems like a good idea at the moment may not actually be that good of an idea when you have time to research and reconsider when emotions are not pressuring you.

Learn to Say No

Perhaps the most valuable tool you will learn in this chapter is the art of saying no. This one goes hand-in-hand with the skill of assertiveness. Considering you were targeted for manipulation; you were likely afraid of confrontation. This, of course, entails saying no to someone. People who hate confrontation hate having to say no to other people. After all, saying no is inherently displeasing, and if you are a people-pleaser, you likely will not like the process. Nevertheless, the best way to avoid being manipulated if you cannot stay away from the manipulator is learning to say no to the manipulator, no matter what strings are being pulled.

When you are saying no to someone, there are three factors to consider—you want your no to be firm, clear, and without excuses. When you are firm, you avoid making too many apologies, and you are not defensive. You can be firm while still being polite, which tells the manipulator that while you recognize that you are not doing what was desired of you, you are not willing to change your mind. By being clear that what you are saying is a no and not a maybe later or to ask you later, the manipulator is aware that your opinion and answer are not changing any time soon. If you make it seem as though you may reconsider in the future, you are going to create even more conflict in the future. Lastly, you want to avoid excuses when you are saying no. You do not have to have a reason to tell someone no; you do not owe anyone an explanation for your reasoning behind declining, and your reason for declining does not invalidate the answer. You are not obligated to do anything that other people are asking of you, no matter how much the manipulator may try to convince you otherwise.

Beyond hitting the above criteria, there are three steps to effectively saying no. First; you must simply say it out loud. You simply say, "No, I'm sorry; I can't help you right now." That is it. If you are not ready to say no at that moment, it is also acceptable to instead say that you want to take some time to reconsider. If even after reconsidering, you cannot think of a way to make it work, or you simply do not want to make it work, you can offer to say yes to something else instead. You can let the other person know that while you cannot do what they have requested, you can help in another way, and offer up that other way in return.

Ask if Request is Reasonable

The last technique you can use to immediately challenge manipulation as it happens is to turn things back around on the manipulator. If the manipulator is really insisting that you do something and will not accept any of the other methods you have used to try to tell the manipulator that you cannot help at that time, you can try turning things around by asking if the request seems reasonable. The manipulator will most likely confirm that it is, in fact, reasonable, at which point, you should ask the manipulator if it would be reasonable to make that same request back to you. The manipulator is now stuck between either doing what he wanted himself or admitting that the request was not actually reasonable in the first place.

For example, imagine that your manipulative partner has been insisting that you should spend an extra two hours that night preparing something for a potluck that he did not inform you about until that evening. He did not get any of the ingredients for the item he wants you to cook, nor did he give you any warning before you got home from your own job, exhausted after working full time. Your partner then assumes that you will have no problems going to the store to get the ingredients, come home, cook dinner, clean up dinner, then cook the potluck dish, clean up that mess, and somehow still get the kids finished with their homework and sent to bed on time. Of course, your partner will sit on the couch and complain about how tired he is after his long day at the desk at work while you somehow attempt to juggle everything.

In this instance, you could stop and ask your partner if it is reasonable to expect all of that all at once. Chances are, your partner will say that, of course, it is reasonable and that you are better at cooking, and he has already told all of his coworkers that he is bringing in that particular dish cooked by you, which has been a huge hit at past potlucks before. Instead of asking how he could help, he assumes you will go along with everything. At this point, you could ask that he does it instead, and when he balks, you tell him that you cannot do it for the same reasons he cannot—you are tired and busy after work, and you still have kids to get ready for bed and school.

Chapter 10: Intermittent Reinforcement

Intermittent reinforcement is incredibly common in relationships that are laden with manipulation and abuse, and it is incredibly dangerous when used effectively. This tactic is designed almost entirely to ensure that you maintain your love and affection for your abusive or manipulative partner, even after your partner has made it clear that he or she is dangerous.

It becomes a dangerous game in which the manipulator knows that he can get away with essentially anything short of murder so long as he shows remorse and a desire to change at least a little bit. This tactic is used by manipulators everywhere in an attempt to keep people on board and interested in relationships when the abuse begins to go t00 far.

Defining Intermittent Reinforcement

Intermittent reinforcement works off of the idea discovered in 1956 by the well-known psychologist B.F. Skinner. He was primarily interested in the idea of reinforcement, and he discovered that ultimately, the best way to encourage good behavior is through inconsistent rewarding as opposed to consistently rewarding at certain points in time. Consistent rewards at predictable intervals were found to eventually taper off as they were no longer interesting. When you know exactly how hard you have to work for something, you do not work hard. You know exactly what you will need to do, and that is it.

With intermittent reinforcement, however, you never know when you will be reinforced, and because of that, you strive to achieve that reinforcement more enthusiastically, hoping you will get it. That sense of anticipation and hope keeps you trying to get that reward even though you know that it is somewhat sporadic.

That same principle can be applied in relationships in which one party is abusive or manipulative—if the manipulator intermittently apologizes, cries, and promises to do better, the victim is more likely to continue to stay behind. The abuse will be tolerated for the moments of affection and the personality that likely attracted the victim in the first place. Because the victim cannot predict when the reinforcement will occur, the victim will constantly seek it out. The victim tries even harder to maintain the relationship through the abuse, seeking out those tiny glimpses of remorse or affection. In the end, the victim is essentially addicted to the thrill that is felt every time the victim attempts to get the end result.

Using Intermittent Reinforcement

Think of this process like those blind bags or loot boxes that kids love these days—you put in some money, and you get an end result. Some of the rewards are rarer than others, but the anticipation of a rare reward keeps you coming back in hopes of getting it. The same thing happens to the victims in the relationship with an abuser utilizing intermittent reinforcement.

When using this, the manipulator will periodically, usually when he or she senses the victim is reaching a breaking point that could lead to the end of the relationship as a whole, will attempt to draw the victim back in through tears, flowers, gifts, affection, and even lavish trips in order to prove his or her love. Through the tears, there will be promises that will never be kept, and through the snot will be the assurances that things can and will get better. However, after a short period of time, the manipulator slips right back into those old, dangerous habits. In the end, the manipulator is able to get away with anything, so long as there is another return back to the intermittent affection.

For example, imagine that you have a manipulative spouse. You love your spouse, but you struggle to deal with the constant manipulation. You are constantly put down and told that you are not good enough, and despite your best efforts to keep him happy, your spouse is frequently telling you that you need to try harder. You eventually fight back, telling your spouse that you are not okay with that kind of treatment, and in response, you get even more manipulation and abuse taken out on you. You are left shocked as a result, never expecting him to go that far. You feel hurt, manipulated, betrayed, and unhappy, and just as those feelings begin to motivate you to get out of the relationship and leave, he comes back. He apologizes to you and tells you that it will never happen again. You want to believe him because you love him and you have built a life with him. You know that a divorce is a long, messy battle that you would rather avoid. The more your spouse begs for forgiveness; the more tempting forgiveness becomes to you. You revel in the affection that follows and the period of calm and good that follows. Unfortunately, however, after a short period of time, the cycle reverts right back to the beginning, and you begin to notice your spouse being short and manipulative again.

Dangers of Intermittent Reinforcement

The biggest problem with intermittent reinforcement is the fact that the victim is essentially addicted to the abuse. The cycle of abuse follows four easily recognizable stages—the period of tensions that build up, the incident of abuse, the stage of reconciliation, which is where intermittent reinforcement occurs, and lastly, the period of calm.

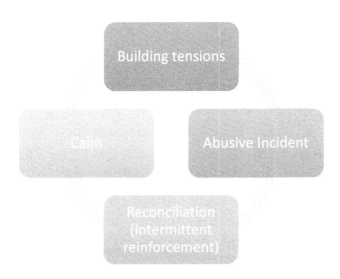

When that unpredictability becomes an addiction, the victim is constantly seeking out the reconciliation stage. Of course, the reconciliation comes with decreasing frequency as the relationship progresses and eventually may even stop appearing altogether. The manipulator gets what he or she wants—a willing participant to the abuse, and the victim risks everything.

This kind of abuse cycle can cause some serious problems, particularly if the couple shares children, as children should be nowhere near a cycle such as this. Nevertheless, the victim finds it grows increasingly more difficult to leave as time goes by, and the manipulator comes to find that even more extreme behavior is acceptable, so long as there is a sorry slapped on the end of it. This means that behavior escalates as it occurs, and eventually, someone can get seriously injured.

The victim sees the instability of the entire situation and has hope from the small tokens of kindness and the affection that occasionally occurs, and that hope is enough to keep the victim trying. The victim knows that the loving person is in there somewhere, buried under hurt or a need to be loved, and the victim develops pity. The pity for the abuser can be used to justify nearly any behavior, explaining away abuse and manipulation as being the unfortunate result of a bad upbringing or a bad trauma. That sympathy keeps the victims present, searching for any signs of that loving person that is nothing more than a tool to keep him or her in line in the first place.

The bond that develops, a bond of trauma and abuse, creates a victim that is fiercely protective of the abuser, constantly trying to explain the abusive tendencies away to ensure that the abuser is protected. The victim then finds himself or herself stuck into a cycle of self-doubt and loathing, wondering why things are so bad as the abuse occurs. Even worse is that oftentimes, these victims then turn to their abusers for any support needed. Because the victims love their abusers, they naturally gravitate toward them for support, despite the fact that there is abuse occurring. The abuse goes completely missed—the victim sees the abuse as little more than unintentional actions that can be fixed while the abuser sees no reason to try changing anything at all when things are working just fine as they are.

Ultimately the only way to break that cycle of abuse is through severing the relationship altogether, something that many abuse victims are not yet ready for. Until a victim is ready to break the cycle on his or her own, that cycle will continue to be prominent and will not be able to be broken. It will not be until the victim is ready to acknowledge just how complex and difficult the entire relationship has been that there will actually be any healing. The victim must be able to acknowledge that there is no benefit to continuing toward the negative relationship and constant cycle of abuse, and must be able to recognize that the constant gamble of when there will be any positive interaction is no longer worthwhile. Only then will the victim break free and see that there is so much more to life than simply waiting for the next scrap of affection to tide him or her over through the abuse.

Chapter 11: Tips and Tricks to Defend Yourself from Manipulation

Do you feel as though no matter how hard you try; you still find manipulators beelining for you? You may try to work on yourself, attempting the steps to neutralize manipulation before it can get to you, but you still find yourself swatting off those pesky attempts left and right. Luckily for you, there is, in fact, a way that you can defend yourself from manipulation, and as you do so, you will become a less attractive target over time. After all, the manipulator wants an easy target, so all you should really have to do to make yourself less interesting to manipulators is to make yourself a less rewarding target.

Today is the day you will learn how to do exactly that—there are eight tips and tricks provided to you here in this chapter that will help you defend yourself from manipulation. Each of these tricks will help you to better protect yourself whenever manipulation attempts start to rear their ugly heads, and if you can master each of these, you will be able to shield yourself from nearly anything the manipulator can possibly throw at you.

Create and Uphold Boundaries

Boundaries are crucial if you want to be able to protect yourself. These are healthy in any and all contexts—there is not a relationship alive that would benefit from not having access to some sort of protection through boundaries. Think of boundaries as the fence you erect around yourself to protect yourself from intruders or being stepped on. You have certain boundaries, certain guidelines for how you would like to be treated, and you expect those around you to follow those specific boundaries. You want to ensure that you are not being stomped on or having your emotions toyed with, and you do this by creating these protective boundaries for yourself. These boundaries can be literally anything—when you are trying to identify what kinds of boundaries you would like to set; it is up to you to come up with what matters to you. Ask yourself how you want to be treated. Do you want people to call you names? If that is a no, write down name-calling under your list of boundaries. Do you want to be hit or otherwise abused? No? Write that down. Do you want people to only address you as Lady Banana Man? That may be a strange, unconventional, and largely comical decision to make, but you are within your rights to declare how you would like to be referred to. Ultimately, it is on you to decide what people call you and what you are willing to respond to, so if your heart says that you want to be Lady Banana Man, you can create a boundary that you will only interact with people who address you appropriately. Your boundaries do not have to make sense to other people—they simply have to make you feel taken care of and respected. Beyond that, any boundaries you set are your own.

When you are setting boundaries, however, you need to make sure that you are willing to enforce them. Are you willing to argue with friends and family over being called

Lady Banana Man? If it is not something that you can legitimately imagine yourself arguing over, it is likely not worth attempting to enforce. On a more serious note, however, when you do attempt to enforce a boundary and have a specific consequence that you threaten if your boundary is not, in fact, honored, you must be willing to follow through. You need to ensure that you are always behaving consistently and following through with whatever you threaten to do, or you are doing nothing but cheapening your boundaries. They do not matter if you refuse to enforce them, after all.

As a more serious example, imagine that you enforce a boundary with your manipulative friend, claiming that you refuse to follow engage in a conversation the next time you hear your friend attempt to demean you. The next time your friend talks down about you, you need to make it a point to separate from the entire situation and disengage. You take some time to yourself at this point, refusing to engage with your friend. When you do engage again, explain that your actions were a direct result of the fact that she could not respect your own beliefs and desires, and because of that, you felt that you had to disengage. Remind her that if she belittles you again, you will once again end contact. Each time you have to end contact, make sure that you make the break between contact a little bit longer. The break is not so much to punish the friend as much as it is to ensure that you are able to get over the violation of your own boundary. You are essentially giving yourself a mini time out from the situation to prevent yourself from blowing up or growing irrationally angry.

Develop a Solid Self-Esteem

The next method of protecting yourself from manipulation is creating solid self-esteem. This is much easier said than done, but it is so incredibly crucial to ensure that you are taken care of. Remember, manipulators look for people with already-fragile self-esteem, and they make it a point to destroy the self-esteem they can touch. For that reason, creating your own solid foundation is a fantastic way to avoid any sort of manipulation in your own future.

When you are developing better self-esteem, one of the best ways of doing so is engaging in self-care. By making self-care a priority for you, you are essentially pledging yourself to make sure you are taken care of. You are telling yourself that you are worthy of care, and in doing so, you remind yourself that you do, in fact, have value despite the fact that the manipulators in your life have been desperate to convince you otherwise thus far.

Beyond self-care, you should attempt to engage in affirmations—small sentences that you tell yourself that remind you that you are, in fact, valuable and worthy of support. Make it a point to allow these affirmations to replace any negativity in your life, ensuring that self-criticism is eliminated. You will find yourself far happier if you manage to do so.

Foster Strong Relationships

Remember, another method that manipulators used was isolating people from their support networks. The best way to combat this is by fostering strong relationships altogether. When you foster these stronger relationships, you ensure that you are far more likely to maintain those relationships, even in the face of adversity or when any manipulators come your way in an attempt to sway you from them. You want to ensure that your relationships with others are strong enough to withstand tactics to alienate you.

Further, when you are in a relationship, make it a point to remember that there is no reason for you to stop investing in relationships with others. Despite the fact that you may be in a newfound relationship, you should absolutely still maintain relationships with friends and family. In fact, you should use them as a way to double-check that anyone you attempt to create a relationship with is actually save. In doing so, you ensure that you are able to protect yourself simply because you keep yourself surrounded by others. Without that isolation necessary, the manipulator cannot manipulate you as completely.

Learn Your Rights

Remember, as a human being; you are entitled to several basic human rights. In knowing your rights, you can ensure that others are not infringing upon them, and if people are, you are now aware of the fact that your rights were infringed upon in the first place simply because you now know what to look for. This is fantastic—it enables you to ensure that any rights you have are actually being honored, which is a great gauge to whether there is any undetected manipulation occurring in your life at the moment. You have several human rights, and this section will highlight the most relevant rights to avoiding manipulation. However, you must recognize that this is not a comprehensive list and if you are interested in a comprehensive list, you will need to look elsewhere.

- **Right to respect:** Everyone deserves to be respected, no matter who they are, what their jobs are, and why they are in a certain situation. Even criminals should be treated with a certain level of respect. You are no exception yourself. Make sure you enforce this right.

- **Right to express yourself:** You have the right to decide how to express your own thoughts, feelings, and opinions, and no one can decide on that for you (within reason). The manipulator cannot decide to take over your thoughts or feelings for you—they are yours to choose and act upon.

- **Right to prioritize yourself:** You deserve to set your own priorities, including setting yourself as a top priority. After all, if you will not make yourself your top priority, who will?

- **Right to say no:** You are well within your rights to tell other people no to requests, and you deserve to be able to do so without any guilt.

- **Right to your own opinions:** You have the right to develop your own opinions, no matter how unpopular or detrimental one person may decide they are. The opinions are your own.

- **Right to protect yourself:** You have a right to ensure that your body and mind are free from physical, mental, and emotional harm. You can ensure that you are taken care of simply because you recognize that you are deserving of that safety.

- **Right to happiness and healthiness:** You deserve happiness and healthiness in life, and you reserve the right to remove anyone who threatens or challenges the ability to create that happiness and healthiness.

Refuse to Make Excuses

When you are interacting with a manipulator and find yourself making excuses, just stop. Yes, your manipulative partner may have had an awful childhood, but that does not give him the excuse to manipulate or abuse you. Yes, your partner may be having a bad day, but that does not excuse it either. Sometimes, people will say things they do not mean out of anger or disappointment, but those people will also oftentimes go back and apologize unprompted because they feel bad about it. Manipulators do not apologize unless it benefits them. When you feel as though you are being manipulated, do not try to make excuses because there are none. There is no reason for a manipulator to treat you poorly, and the less you try to justify the abuse and manipulation, the better. Instead, make it a point to call out the manipulation as directly and unemotionally as possible without attempting to excuse the behaviors.

Set Consequences

Remember that consequences are important, and you need to ensure you set them to protect yourself. You deserve to create boundaries that are respected, and you are well within your rights to set a consequence for any and all attempts to override your own boundaries. For example, if someone violates a boundary, you can choose to take a break from that relationship until thinking about the violation of the boundary is no longer infuriating to you. If you have a manipulative parent that cannot stop attempting to manipulate you and your own children, it makes sense that you would attempt to limit contact between your young children and your manipulative parents that are attempting to subject your children to that kind of manipulation in the first place.

Remember, these consequences are not so much about punishing the other person as they are about regaining the necessary distance to enable you to protect and enforce your own boundaries. Remember your rights—you are deserving of happiness, and you are deserving of protecting yourself from harm. You are doing exactly that in this situation when you create a consequence, no matter what it is. If you cancel an event that you invited the manipulator to, so be it. If you had to stop attempting to salvage the relationship because the manipulator would not respect your boundaries, so be it. The important part is you protect yourself.

Reject Blame and Personalization

Remember, manipulators will constantly attempt to utilize blame and personalization in order to control you. They will make you feel as though everything is your own fault and that you should feel bad for it. They may claim even the most outrageous things are your fault, such as it is your fault that it rained that day because you did not do the rain dance enough the night prior. Remember, it is not your fault and should never be treated as such. Instead, recognize that any attempts to blame you are manipulation and reject them.

When it comes to personalization, you are essentially taking something that was said to heart. If the manipulator says you are selfish, you may feel as though you are selfish—that is personalization, even though the reality is that you are not selfish, and in fact, are the exact opposite. Nevertheless, you cannot help but feel selfish after being called as such. If you want to break from that cycle, you must learn to stop caring about what people are saying about you. Instead of getting worked up about it, you decide to focus on the fact that the other person is a manipulator and does not deserve to be considered a credible individual. Rather than allowing the manipulator to make you feel bad, you simply reject the opinion altogether, recognizing that it is not likely to be credible considering the source.

Maintain Flexibility

Lastly, when you are engaging with a manipulator, remember to be flexible. Manipulators love to survive people. They will suddenly engage in unpredictable behaviors in an attempt to through you off because when you are surprised and unsure about something, you are more easily swayed. Remember to expect the unexpected when dealing with manipulators, and you will be just fine. You can maintain this flexibility relatively simply—remind yourself that anything can happen, and you will be able to figure out a way around it. If you trust yourself and your own instincts, you will be fine.

Conclusion

Congratulations, you have made it to the end of *Covert Manipulation*. It has been a long journey through several different topics that were hopefully of the utmost use to you. Hopefully, they have provided you with several of the necessary tools you will need to achieve the goals that had motivated you to purchase and read this book in the first place.

As you read through this book, you were introduced to several different topics that were meant to benefit you. You learned about the insidious covert manipulation and how it is frequently used. You took a look at why people use these manipulation tactics, as well as how to identify whether you have become a victim of abuse yourself. You have learned about several different emotional manipulation tactics, walking you through the steps of several, as well as how to influence people without manipulation tactics. Next, you took a look at what manipulation in relationships and workplaces looks like, as well as how to eliminate it altogether.

From here, you have several options: You can continue your reading of forms of manipulation. You can continue to develop your knowledge in order to get a solid working foundation on how to control other people. You could look toward dark psychology for more information about covert manipulation. On the other hand, you could delve into emotional intelligence to develop natural social skills that are influential without being manipulative. You could even focus on some books about persuasion.

Perhaps your next step is to put the skills you have learned to use; you may find yourself surrounded by manipulators you were unaware of in your life that you recognize after getting a chance to view the signs of manipulation. You may have decided that you were going to evict all of the manipulators from your life once and for all. Regardless of what you will do next, you will do so with skill.

Remember, the most important aspect of this book to remember is that ultimately, when you are attempting to change the mind of someone else, the most important factor is the intention. Intention can be the difference between manipulation that is unethical and possibly even illegal, and persuasion, which is largely safe to use in workplaces, particularly in business settings. Ultimately, the tools within this book were provided for your own education, and how you choose to wield them is on you. Remember that these skills come with their own level of responsibility and that you are tasked with ensuring that you do not use these skills harmfully.

Lastly, as you close up this book, if you found it useful at all, an Amazon review would be greatly appreciated. Thank you for your interest in *Covert Manipulation,* and hopefully, it serves you well.

Made in the USA
Monee, IL
07 January 2023

24665939R00075